San Francisco Peninsula Birdwatching

Sequoia Audubon Society

with members of the Golden Gate Audubon Society

Dedicated to that world traveler from Europe who chose to be with us in the winters of his young life — *Mergus albellus.*

The descriptions of Golden Gate Park, the Presidio, Lake Merced, and Lands End are revisions of articles originally appearing in *The Gull,* the monthly newsletter of the Golden Gate Audubon Society. Maps by Nancy Conzett originally appeared in *The Gull.*

Cover: Hooded Merganser by Cliff Richer

ISBN 0-9614301-0-9
Published by Sequoia Audubon Society
         P.O. Box 1131
         Burlingame, CA 94011

Copies may be ordered from the publisher.

Editor

Anne Scanlan-Rohrer

Publication Committee

Rick Baird   Chip Haven   Donna Kirsacko   Peter Metropulos
Cliff Richer   Tom Taber   Anne Scanlan-Rohrer

Contributors

Sequoia Audubon Society:

Jean and Frank Allen	Sharon Hom	Cliff Richer
Rick Baird	Donna Kirsacko	Wilma Rockman
Wanda Belland	Peter Metropulos	Scott Smithson
Nick Coiro	Donna L. Peterson	Tom Taber

Golden Gate Audubon Society:

Alan Hopkins   Dan Murphy   Mary Louise Rosegay

Ornithological Advisor

Peter Metropulos

Illustrations

Andrea Hom   Cliff Richer   Anne Scanlan-Rohrer

Maps

Nancy Conzett   Andrea Hom   Donna Kirsacko

General Assistance

Mary Bresler   Elgin Juri   Scot Rohrer   Betty Wyatt

Proofreader

Mary Roach

Layout

Mary Roach   Scot Rohrer

CONTENTS

INTRODUCTION

The San Francisco Peninsula encompasses a large variety of avian habitats in a relatively compact space. The urban corridor of cities comprising San Mateo and San Francisco counties is surrounded by the waters of San Francisco Bay and the Pacific Ocean on three sides; the fourth side, the southern end of the peninsula, is abundant in wooded parks and open grassland. Over 370 species of birds have been found in this area, ranging from backyard Scrub Jays and Chestnut-backed Chickadees to rare vagrant passerines in Golden Gate Park and the exotic Smew that began wintering in Foster City in the 1980's. To be able to drive from San Francisco, the cosmopolitan center of culture and finance, to the south coast beaches and Pescadero Marsh in 90 minutes is one of the many reasons why this area is so appealing to people in general and birders in particular.

This book is intended to be a guide to the known and not-so-well-known birding spots in San Mateo County and San Francisco. It was written by members of the Sequoia Audubon Society, with contributions from members of the Golden Gate Audubon Society. Birders can be all ages, shapes, and sizes, and the contributors to this book are no exception. The description of San Pedro Valley County Park was originally to be written by Gil West, Sequoia's 74-years-young super-birder and member of the California "400 Club" (over 400 species seen in California in one year). Gil's impending birding trip to China prevented him from completing the task, so he gave it to his trusted and experienced birding associate — 11-year-old Scott Smithson. This exemplifies the differences that can and do exist between our local birders; however, the contributors to this book all share enthusiasm for their subjects, as well as many combined years of experience.

One other important factor that all peninsula birders share is concern for the environment and apprehension over its rapid decline. Several of the sites described in this book were in an unstable state at the time of printing, threatened by development or neglect. If the different habitats found on the San Francisco Peninsula are not continually watched over and protected by those who care for the richness of life in all its forms, there will be increasingly fewer swamps to slog through and woods to wander in; the decline of wildlife itself will leave little joy in birdwatching. The serious reality of environmental protection must always preface the fun aspects of birdwatching, if those joyous moments are to remain.

— Anne Scanlan-Rohrer
September 1984

Bewick's Wren — Andrea Hom

General Guidelines

- Respect private property at all times.

- Be aware of ticks, poison oak, rattlesnakes, and eroding cliff edges, not necessarily in that order.

- Proper attire and equipment can make a big difference in the enjoyment level of any birdwatching outing. Good binoculars and a spotting scope, sturdy waterproof shoes, and a warm wind-resistant jacket are worth every dollar paid for them.

- The Sequoia Audubon Society publishes a *Checklist of the Birds of San Mateo County.* This checklist was updated and revised in 1984. The chapter also provides checklists for Foster City and Pescadero Marsh. Contact the chapter office, 415-593-7368, Box 1131, Burlingame, CA, 94011, to obtain checklists. San Mateo County also provides a checklist for the birds of Memorial Park.

- Every attempt was made to make this guide as current as possible. However, the information provided here is subject to change. The Sequoia Audubon Society is not responsible for changes in information provided here. The book will be revised periodically.

- Public transportation information for individual areas was provided by contributors where known; do not assume that none exists for an area if it is not mentioned. The San Mateo County Transit District (SamTrans) and MUNI of San Francisco provide routes to many areas and should be contacted if further information on specific routes is desired.

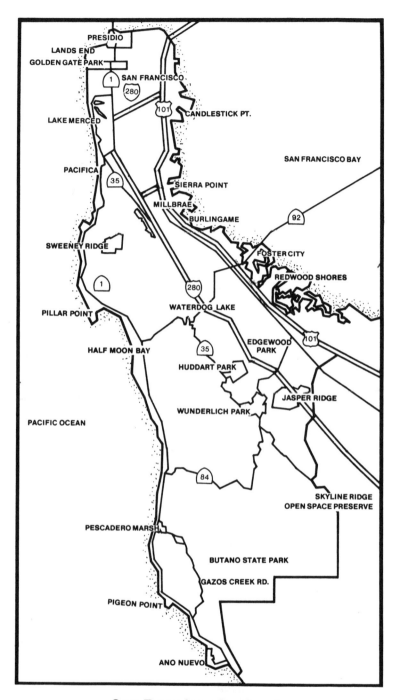

San Francisco Peninsula

SAN FRANCISCO

San Francisco has been described with a multitude of super-latives regarding its unique mixture of culture, cuisines, and overall ambience. Birders visiting the city for its other attractions will not be disappointed by the abundance of bird species in several open areas within the city limits.

Most of the best birding areas are on the west side of the city, near or on the Pacific Ocean. Public transportation is available from downtown San Francisco to these areas; call MUNI or BART for information about the most current routes and schedules. A San Francisco street and transit map is available in many down-town bookstores.

A culinary note: one of the best ways to end a solid day of birding is with a satisfying meal at a good restaurant. San Francisco has been said to have more restaurants per capita than any other American city. Some of the best restaurants are near the prime birding spots; check a city restaurant guide or ask local birders for their recommendations.

Golden Gate Park

San Francisco's Golden Gate Park is among the finest urban parks in the world. It is wholly manmade except for land forms and a few oak groves in the eastern part of the park. Among its many fine features are extensive plantings of Monterey pine, Monterey cypress, and several eucalyptus species; over a dozen lakes and ponds; an interesting and varied avifauna; and the exhibits and collections of the California Academy of Sciences.

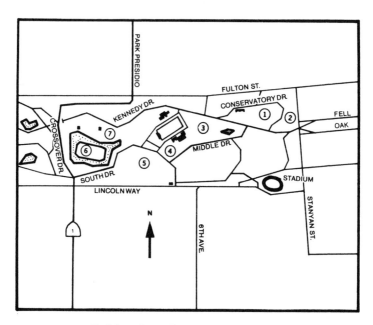

Golden Gate Park — Eastern Developed Area

The park is divided into two parts: the developed area east of Crossover Drive and the less developed area west of it. Generally speaking, the western naturalistic area provides the best birding habitats, though there are many fine spots in the eastern part of the park.

The Eastern Developed Area — Stanyan Street to Crossover Drive

The Fuschia Garden (#1), located on Conservatory Drive East, provides excellent habitat for Allen's Hummingbirds in spring and summer. Anna's Hummingbirds are present all year. Sparrows, finches, and Scrub Jays are also permanent residents. The oak grove (#2), east of this area, is said to have records for migrants uncommon to the city, but generally speaking, both areas are rather slow and the number of species likely to be seen is limited.

The Rhododendron Dell (#3) is located east of the Academy of Sciences and south of Kennedy Drive and 6th Avenue. During the fall it has been known to attract a variety of vagrants and migrants. *Empidonax* flycatchers occur here regularly in fall as do Olive-sided Flycatchers and Western Wood-Pewees. Be sure to watch the "pigeons" in this area because they are not all Rock Doves. A large flock of Band-tailed Pigeons can frequently be seen in the Monterey pines and cypress over the rhododendrons. This is

6

probably the most regular spot in the park for that species.

There are other dells and groves in this area which may or may not be productive birding sites, but they are not birded with enough regularity to merit discussion here.

While in the area be sure to stop at the California Academy of Sciences (#4). There, you may see dioramas of California bird habitats as well as a collection of stuffed birds likely to be seen in somewhat better conditions outside the confines of the museum.

Strybing Arboretum

Strybing Arboretum (#5) is by far the most diverse plant community in the park. From its beginning under the direction of John McLaren and Eric Walther in 1937, the Arboretum has not only housed an excellent botanical exhibit but has offered interesting birding as well. Check the pond near the entrance across the street from the Japanese Tea Garden for a Eurasian Wigeon during the winter. The pond generally has an interesting flock of ducks, geese, and swans, many of which are exotics. Walk the path paralleling the fence to the left of the entrance gate. Red-breasted and Red-naped (Yellow-bellied) Sapsuckers have wintered in this area. There does not seem to be a best way to bird the Arboretum. While following any of the many paths watch for California Quail, Hermit and Varied Thrushes, and Rufous-sided Towhee. The mixed flocks of chickadees, Bushtits, and kinglets sometimes are joined by Hermit and Townsend's Warblers.

Stow Lake

Stow Lake (#6) is the most widely used lake in the park. The walk around it is about three quarters of a mile. The island in the middle, Strawberry Hill, is accessible by two bridges. A dirt path circles it and winds its way to the top. A small snack bar and boat rental facility are located at the northwest corner of the lake. Restrooms may be found behind the building.

Check the area around the concession for gulls and ducks. Ring-necked Ducks may be seen here in winter. A large flock of Brewer's Blackbirds inhabits the small island near this area. Walk east until the road straightens out and check the eucalyptus trees across the street for any of a variety of birds, including fall migrants such as Western Tanagers and various warblers. Since this area is seldom birded, there is no telling what might show up. In January 1978, a Tennessee Warbler was found here. (See the section on Pioneer Log Cabin [#7] for further information.) Continue to check the row of trees until the road turns to the right. The trail leading down the hill goes to the Japanese Tea Garden.

Ring-necked Duck — Cliff Richer

The flock of ducks at this point on the lake generally includes Mallards, American Wigeons, Lesser Scaups, and Ruddy Ducks. A Tufted Duck wintered in this area in 1972. As you continue around the lake listen for the common birds which inhabit this and all other areas of the park. Among others you may hear Belted Kingfisher, Scrub Jay, and Northern Flicker.

Once the area between Strawberry Hill and Prayerbook Cross to the north was a rock quarry which provided much of the material used in street construction in the city. The reconstructed Huntington Falls on the northeast side of the island and the few remaining palm trees are reminders of the Victorian era which saw construction of structures such as the Conservatory and events such as the Midwinter Fair of 1894. During the fall, winter, and spring the island is home for a large number of sparrows and juncos. Allen's and Anna's Hummingbirds reside on the island and Scrub Jays can usually be found here. During the fall, migrants seem to be attracted to the island. Vagrants may occur among the flocks composed primarily of Yellow-rumped Warblers.

Adjacent to Stow Lake is the Pioneer Log Cabin (#7), which is situated on the edge of a meadow with a nice picnic area and excellent birding habitat. Not only do the trees here change with the seasons, but variations in light, wind, and fog conditions make this among the most visually attractive locations in the park. A wonderful variety of migrants such as Western Tanager, Wilson's ,and Yellow Warblers, and Western Flycatcher are regular visitors. There are also records for American Redstart, Blackpoll Warbler, and Bay-breasted Warbler. This certainly seems to be a spot which attracts a great enough variety of birds to merit extensive birding. Walk behind the cabin and follow the dirt paths which follow the contour of the hill. The most productive area is the hillside behind the picnic area, but similar habitat exists along the south edge of the meadow for its entire length.

The Western Undeveloped Area —
Crossover Drive to the Great Highway

The western part of the park is less structured than the eastern section. The forest here provides a windbreak for the more formal plantings to the east. It lends itself to more leisurely walks and birding experiences than the previously described areas.

Elk Glen (#8), Mallard (#9), and Metson (#10) Lakes
The area north of Lincoln Way between Crossover Drive and the Sunset Boulevard entrance to the park can provide excellent birding. The eucalyptus, pine, and cypress forest opens at several meadows and envelops three lovely lakes. Here you can find areas of solitude and unique beauty. To bird the area adequately plan on walking around each lake, going off the beaten path into meadows and through the forest, and following bridle paths instead of the streets.

A good place to start is Elk Glen Lake. Located at the foot of the 25th Avenue entrance on South Drive, this is generally the most regular site in the park for Wood Ducks. There is little vegetation

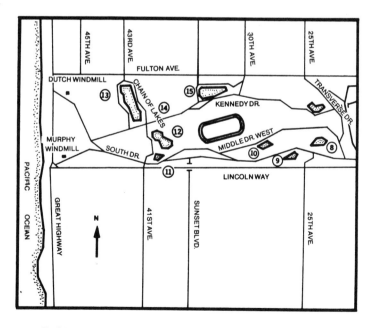

Golden Gate Park — Western Undeveloped Area

around the lake's edge, but the area is good for finches and sparrows, including the locally unusual Lincoln's Sparrow. The trees usually have a flock of Chestnut-backed Chickadees and Pygmy Nuthatches. Walk around the lake and return to South Drive where you should turn right. A more secluded trail is the bridle path across the street.

Mallard Lake is on the south side of South Drive between 25th Avenue and Sunset Boulevard. This is a fine duck feeding pond. There always seems to be plenty of Mallards, American Wigeons, coots, and gulls present from early fall until mid-spring. Ring-necked Ducks, Lesser Scaup, and an occasional Common Goldeneye winter here. Land birds can be found around the back side of the lake. They may include Black Phoebe, Red-breasted Sapsucker and, with a lot of luck, Red Crossbills. Like much of the park, Mallard Lake is under-birded and may be a far richer birding site than most of us realize.

From Mallard Lake continue west. If you're on foot, walk to the 30th Avenue entrance to the park. A path comes down the hill from the left and continues on to the right. Follow the path to the right as it goes through a valley. About 200 yards to the right is Metson Lake. If you're driving, continue west, take the first right turn, then turn right again in about 200 yards. Continue to the top of the hill to Metson Lake.

This little pond is a regular spot for Wood Ducks. They have been seen here during all months of the year, though they are much less frequently present during the summer months. Mew Gulls and a variety of ducks including Northern Shoveler are usually present during the fall, winter, and spring. Check the trees on the south side of the lake for Hermit and Varied Thrushes, Pygmy Nuthatch, and woodpeckers. The valley south of the lake is good for California Quail, sparrows, and other species. Keep an eye on the sky for accipiters and Red-tailed Hawk.

From Metson Lake continue along Middle Drive West (keep to the right) until it ends at Transverse Drive; turn right and turn right again at South Drive for the return to Elk Glen Lake. If on foot, there are a number of alternate routes which can be taken. Walk from the south side of the lake to the valley below and go left to the end of the valley. Follow the dirt road to the right until it reaches South Drive and then walk to the left to Elk Glen Lake.

Chain of Lakes

The Chain of Lakes transects the park between 41st Avenue and Lincoln Way and 43rd Avenue and Fulton Street. These three lakes

Wood Duck — Cliff Richer

provide one of the best and most popular birding sites in the park. Varied habitats appear to be the key to this as a valuable birding and natural site. Recent redevelopment of these three lakes has preserved much of their natural value. Though they were deepened and sealed, and much of the marsh vegetation was removed, they continue to provide wetland habitat for the largest variety of birds in the park.

South Lake (#11)

Though generally unproductive during the summer, South Lake is good for ducks in other seasons. It usually harbors a number of Mallards, American Wigeons, and coots. Look here for Lesser Scaup, Common Goldeneye, and Eurasian Wigeon as well. The shrubs and trees on the west side of the lake may harbor Varied and Hermit Thrushes, Chestnut-backed Chickadees, and a variety of other small birds including occasional vagrants. The vegetation to the east is dense, difficult to walk through, and therefore seldom birded.

Middle Lake (#12)

Middle Lake (#12) is among the most productive areas to bird in Golden Gate Park. During the fall, Virginia and Sora Rails may be heard from the marshes. A large variety of warblers, sparrows, thrushes, and other small birds feed along its edge. The eucalyptus and Monterey pines on the southwest side of the lake are favored by fall migrants (e.g., Western Tanagers, Nashville, MacGillivray's, and Townsend's Warblers) as well as some rather interesting vagrants (Black-throated Blue Warbler, American Redstart, Tennessee Warbler, Rose-breasted Grosbeak, Summer Tanager, etc.). Residents likely to be seen throughout the year include Downy Woodpecker, Brown Towhee, Anna's Hummingbird, and Common Yellowthroat. The edges of the lake are a jumble of blackberry briars which provide an abundance of food and excellent refuge for these and other species. Watch for Red-shouldered Hawk overhead.

Continue north along the path to a small meadow. Check here for American Robins, Cedar Waxwings, Pine Siskins, and Bushtits. This area is also good for Golden-crowned Sparrows, Fox Sparrows, Song Sparrows, including some rather unusual subspecies, and occasional Lincoln's Sparrows. Leaving the path, go down into the little redwood grove. This area has been good for fall warblers in the past. It also provides excellent views of Middle Lake.

Continue around the lake. Watch for Western Pond Turtles on rocks and logs above water level. If you notice fins and splotches of muddy water you're seeing one or more of the carp which inhabit the lake. Check the duck flock on the lake for Wood Ducks, Northern Shovelers, and such. A single male Redhead Duck showed up in the fall of 1978.

The eastern side of the lake is excellent for most of the species previously mentioned. It provides fine views of the forested area east of the lake. The area near the California bay tree at the south end of the lake is good for finches, towhees, and sparrows.

North Lake (#13)

From the western side of Middle Lake follow the trail north, crossing Kennedy Drive and Chain of Lakes Drive East. Walk west about 30 yards to the path that leads down a short steep hill to the right. Circle the lake to the left. Chestnut-backed Chickadees, Bushtits, Hutton's Vireo, and warblers can frequently be found in the trees overhanging the path. Within about 100 yards the path turns to the right and crosses a small bridge. This area is good for Varied, Hermit, and Swainson's Thrushes, Purple Finch, and a variety of fall and spring vagrants including American Redstart, Tennessee Warbler, and Northern Waterthrush. Some records for this area go back to the 1930's, making it one of the earliest known sites to see vagrants on the central California coast. Continue around the lake. The marshes provide habitat for Common Yellowthroat, Yellow-rumped Warbler, Song Sparrow, and occasional rails. The willows and bald cypress on the islands should be checked for roosting Black-crowned Night-Herons and Wood Ducks. Watch for Downy Woodpeckers, Red-breasted Sapsuckers, and other woodland species.

Check the shrubs at the north end of the lake for Dark-eyed Junco, Fox Sparrow, and Brown Towhee. Water birds on the lake may include Pied-billed Grebe, Double-crested Cormorant, Mallard, American Wigeon, Bufflehead, Northern Shoveler, and American Coot. Check the flock of gulls for Ring-billed and Thayer's Gulls. Continue along the east side of the lake to the starting point. The broader view from this side of the lake makes it a good place to look for Barn, Cliff, Violet-green, and Tree Swallows. Check the trees across the lake for hawks and other roosting birds including Green-backed Heron.

The wooded plot across Chain of Lakes Drive West from the north end of North Lake provides excellent birding for woodland species. The area is best birded by following the paths which crisscross it. Downy Woodpecker, Northern Flicker, Red-breasted and Pygmy Nuthatches, Brown Creeper, Golden-crowned and Ruby-crowned Kinglets, juncos, finches, and sparrows are among the species which can be found. Red Crossbills use the plot regularly. There are records for Common Barn and Long-eared Owls and Summer Tanager as well. The hedgerow at the western end of the plot, adjacent to the archery field, was used by a Wood Thrush during the winter of 1983-1984. This area seems to have potential as a fall vagrant trap.

Buffalo Paddock

On Kennedy Drive about 100 yards east of Chain of Lakes Drive is the Buffalo Paddock (#14). From Kennedy Drive check the field for sparrows, finches, and blackbirds. Brown-headed Cowbirds can be seen here frequently. There are a few records of Tricolored Blackbirds. A Red-tailed Hawk generally winters in the vicinity of this meadow. There is a water trough on the west side of the hill which is sometimes allowed to overflow. Scan the tall grass between the trough and the meadow for Common Snipe during the wet winter months, though if there is no overflow this will be an exercise in futility. The Buffalo Paddock can be circled on foot. The forest surrounding it is good for Dark-eyed Junco, Pygmy and Red-breasted Nuthatches, Brown Creeper, Yellow-rumped Warbler, and various woodpeckers. Golden-crowned Sparrows can frequently be seen at the east and west ends of the Paddock in vicinities near shrubs. The fact that the meadow is fenced off makes it a unique short grass prairie which is seldom disturbed by man and therefore provides an open, undisturbed area for birds and small mammals needing such habitat.

Spreckles Lake

Just east of the Buffalo Paddock on Kennedy Drive is Spreckles Lake (#15). It is a fine spot for viewing wintering gulls and ducks. Glaucous-winged, Western, California, and Mew Gulls are common here. There are infrequent sightings of Ring-billed, Herring, and Thayer's Gulls. Western and Heermann's Gulls can generally be found here during the summer. The winter duck population includes Mallards, American Wigeons, Ruddy Ducks, Lesser Scaups, and Canvasbacks. Northern Pintails and Greater Scaups can be seen here from time to time. There are several Eurasian Wigeon records for this lake. Check here also for Western and Pied-billed Grebes, Double-crested Cormorants and, less frequently, loons, other grebes, and ducks. Brewer's Blackbirds have been observed swimming, much like phalaropes, on the north side of the lake.

There are also other parts of Golden Gate Park in which to seek birds. Lloyd's Lake on Kennedy Drive can be productive. The trail around it is rather isolated. The Dutch Windmill, Murphy Windmill, and the cypress trees forming the wind break along the Great Highway may also be productive though this area, too, is rather isolated. The footpaths extending from 45th Avenue and Lincoln Way to Middle Lake are good for sparrows. The roads between the eastern side of Spreckles Lake and the 30th Avenue and Fulton Street entrance may also be interesting.

It is important to remember that this site guide is valid for the period from mid-September until the end of April. Between May and early September waterfowl abandon the park for northern breeding areas. Many of the species discussed in this article are absent or in reduced numbers during the summer. If you do bird the park during the summer you may expect to find Downy Woodpecker, Pygmy Nuthatch, Band-tailed Pigeon, Brown Towhee, Brewer's Blackbird, and a variety of sparrows and finches.

Directions: Golden Gate Park may be reached from the north or south on Route 1 (19th Avenue and Park Presidio Boulevard), from the east on Fell Street, or by MUNI routes N, 5, 18, 21, 28, 44, 71, or 72.

Facilities: There are restrooms at the boat rental facility at Stow Lake, near Spreckles Lake by the Model Yacht Clubhouse, and behind the Music Temple at the music concourse (near the Academy of Sciences). There are snack stands at Stow Lake and behind the Music Temple, and restaurants for patrons at the Academy of Sciences and the De Young Museum.

— Dan Murphy

Lands End — Seal Rocks and Lincoln Park

San Francisco's Lands End is an area of breathtaking vistas and dynamic bird life. The rocky cliffs and small beaches make it the best place to observe ocean and shorebirds in San Francisco. However, the most attractive aspect of Lands End is the observation of migrant land birds. On a good day it is possible to see migrant hawks, flycatchers, orioles, tanagers, sparrows, and warblers. During a few days each spring and fall, a "wave" of migrants will pass through and warblers can be seen by the hundreds.

It is possible to check all the best spots in the area by making a large loop of the trails and roads that follow the coast. A good place to start is the dirt parking lot at Merrie Way above the Cliff House and Sutro Baths (#1, 2 on the map). As in most urban parks, it is a good idea to take a friend along and avoid leaving valuables in your car.

Depending on tides, you may decide to begin or finish birding at the Cliff House (#1). The birds are most easily seen here at high tide. The observation deck behind the restaurants is the best place to scan Seal Rocks, which abound with bird life. American Black Oystercatchers, Western Gulls, and Brandt's Cormorants all nest on the rocks. In June the rocks become covered with Brown Pelicans and their cohorts, the Heermann's Gulls. In mid-July the shorebirds begin to reappear; look for Wandering Tattler, Willet, Surfbird, Ruddy and Black Turnstones, and Sanderlings.

After the Cliff House, the next spot to check is the remains of Sutro Baths (#2). Just below the coffee shop is a trail that leads to the old baths. The baths are no longer used by swimmers but are a favorite spot for gulls and shorebirds to drink and bathe. In the

15

Lands End — Seal Rocks and Lincoln Park

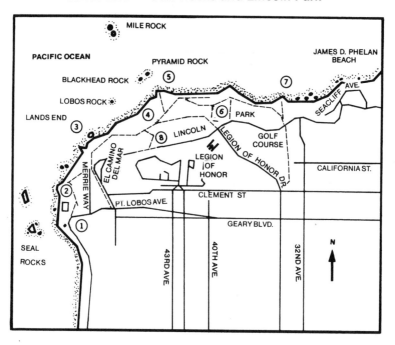

winter small numbers of waterfowl stop on the ponds. Mallards, American Wigeon, Ring-necked Duck, Greater and Lesser Scaup, and Common and sometimes Barrow's Goldeneyes can be seen. Shorebirds not associated with rocky shores such as Black-necked Stilt, Pectoral Sandpiper, and Red and Red-necked Phalaropes are possible around the ponds.

The large flat cement area on the point to the north on the ponds is an excellent spot to scope for seabirds. In fall and winter the ocean becomes alive with Red-throated, Common, and Arctic Loons, Western Grebes, and Surf, White-winged, and Black Scoters. A strong incoming tide produces a choppy rip line where the water from the sea and bay meet. It is along that choppy line where seabird watching is usually the best. Bonaparte's Gulls and Forster's, Caspian, and Elegant Terns come to feed on the rich waters churned up in the rip. Some of the more pelagic birds possible are Parasitic and Pomarine Jaegers, Common Tern, Sooty Shearwater, Northern Fulmar, and Black-legged Kittiwake. Alcids such as Marbled Murrelet and Cassin's Auklet have been found. A sharp eye can usually find a Common Murre every month of the year. Mammals found here include California Sea Lion, Harbor Seal, and, with some luck, Harbor Porpoise during

16

the spring. California Gray Whales can pass within 100 yards of the point.

To continue the loop, check the row of cypress trees at the end of the parking lot for warblers. Follow the trail that heads northeast at the east end of these trees. Keep to the right until the trail meets a dirt road. The road is actually an old trolley car track bed that ran from downtown San Francisco to the Cliff House. The cliffs along tne way can be good for seabird watching. In the summer there are usually a few Pigeon Guillemots on the large rock to the east (#3). In fall and winter the cove created by the rock is a good place to study gulls and terns.

From the view of the rock the trail goes slightly inland. After about a quarter of a mile there is a large grassy open area which is good for finches. This area is the bottom of the "West Wash." As the road bends to the north, watch for the paved road on the right. This road leads to the Palace of the Legion of Honor through Lincoln Park Golf Course. Head up the road only as far as the large willow patch (#4). In the winter the cypress and eucalyptus trees are the most consistent spots for finding Townsend's Warblers at Lands End. The willows are most productive when they bud in the spring, at which time they are swarming with Anna's, Allen's, and some Rufous Hummingbirds; there may also be Bewick's Wrens, Hutton's Vireos, and Purple Finches around. During migration this spot is worth checking for warblers and flycatchers. If you wish to skip spot #5, the paved road is a shortcut to the "East Wash" (#6).

To continue the loop, go back to the dirt road and watch for a trail on the left by some trash cans. This trail goes down to Lands End proper (#5). From the tip of the point there is a fine view of the coast. Scoping the water below Mile Rock has produced Marbled and Ancient Murrelets and is an especially good spot for loons. Closer to shore are Pyramid Rock and Blackhead Rock where Pelagic Cormorants roost. In the winter of 1979 these rocks were frequented by two Harlequin Ducks.

Return to the main road and continue east. After a short distance watch for the new trail that goes up the hill on the right. This trail continues the walk, but in summer you may want to go past it to check the bottom of the sheer cliff for Pigeon Guillemots.

At the top of the new trail are trees that border the "East Wash" (#6). These trees are among the most productive for migrants and have produced rarities; Kentucky Warbler, among others, has been seen here. The "East Wash" is actually an ongoing landslide. In the stormy winter of 1982 the whole area was moved three feet closer to the sea, and the old trail was destroyed in the process. To check the wash, take the trail that leads up the wash as the main trail bends back towards the coast. From the large flat area be sure to check the large fennel (anise) patch. All the trees and shrubs that surround the wash are worth checking since rare birds have been found in almost all of them. Some of the "goodies" that have been found include Hooded, Magnolia, and Blackburnian Warblers, Indigo Buntings, and Rose-breasted Grosbeaks, along with some unusual western birds like Green-tailed Towhee and Common Poorwill.

To go to the next spots, backtrack to the main trail. As the trail rounds the point, the foliage becomes thicker and there are usually Chestnut-backed Chickadees, Bushtits, and Song and White-crowned Sparrows. In the winter they are joined by Golden-crowned and Fox Sparrows and Ruby-crowned and Golden-crowned Kinglets. During migration watch for Western Flycatcher, Orange-crowned and Wilson's Warblers, and Warbling Vireo.

As the trail reaches its end (#7), Lincoln Park Golf Course appears on the right. The open area to the left once had nesting Pygmy Nuthatches and Tree Swallows; unfortunately, the Park Service cut down the trees they nested in. From the cliff's edge look east to James D. Phelan Beach, where Long-billed Curlew, Whimbrel, and Marbled Godwits may be among the Willets and Sanderlings on the beach far below.

Before starting up El Camino Del Mar, check the first 100 yards of the trail which begins directly across the street and runs along the 18th hole green to Legion of Honor Drive at 43rd Avenue. The pine and cypress trees that line the green may have swallows, nuthatches, Brown Creepers, warblers, and possibly Red Crossbills.

There always seems to be bird activity along El Camino Del Mar. Downy Woodpecker, Olive-sided Flycatcher, Tree Swallow, Pygmy Nuthatch, and Dark-eyed Junco have all nested along the road. In the winter Yellow-rumped Warblers are abundant and Townsend's Warblers are fairly common. During spring and fall migration there may be Nashville, Black-throated Gray, and Hermit Warblers. Vagrants like Yellow-throated, Chestnut-sided, and Blackpoll Warblers and Northern Parula have been found in the trees along the road.

At the top of the hill the main road turns in front of the Palace of the Legion of Honor, but continue straight along El Camino Del Mar past the dead end sign. The pines that line the street can be quite productive. Warblers in the tops of the trees can be seen more easily by taking the small road to the left where they can be seen at eye level. There are restrooms at the end of this small road.

At the end of El Camino Del Mar a trail leads to the "West Wash" (#8). On a hot day this spot is a must. There is always a trickle of water running through the willows and they can be filled with birds that have come to drink and bathe. During migration this seems to be a favorite stopping place for Western Flycatcher, Nashville Warbler, and Lazuli Bunting. Specialties like Orchard Oriole, Black-throated Green Warbler, and Swamp Sparrow have stopped here.

To finish the loop, head straight onto the old El Camino Del Mar road bed. There are usually many common birds along the road until it ends at the parking lot at the west end of El Camino Del Mar. From the northwest corner of the parking lot look for the steps that lead back down to the old trolley car bed. From here retrace your steps to the parking lot at Merrie Way.

It may not always be desirable to do this large loop. By parking at the Legion of Honor smaller loops can be made from the trails that run up and down the washes connecting the upper road and lower trail. From season to season you will find Seal Rocks, Lands End, and Lincoln Park ever changing and, for me, ever fascinating.

Directions: From the South Bay, take Interstate 280 north to Skyline Boulevard (Highway 35). Skyline Boulevard becomes the Great Highway near Lake Merced. Follow the Great Highway to the Cliff House. From the north, take Highway 101 through the Presidio to Geary Boulevard and head west. Geary turns off onto Point Lobos Avenue at about 40th Avenue. Point Lobos Avenue ends in front of the Cliff House; shortly before that is Merrie Way. From the East Bay, take Interstate 80 to Highway 101 towards the Civic Center. This exit ends and becomes Franklin Street. Take Franklin Street to Geary and turn left. Take Geary to Point Lobos Avenue at 40th Avenue and continue to Merrie Way and the Cliff House.

Facilities: There are restrooms at the end of the small road near the Legion of Honor as mentioned above, as well as in the back of the Cliff House gift shop. There are restaurants and a snack stand at the Cliff House.

— Alan S. Hopkins

The Presidio of San Francisco

The Presidio of San Francisco is a large parklike area in the northwest corner of the city adjacent to the Golden Gate Bridge. For two centuries it has been a military reservation and has so been inviolate to the spread of urban development. Large tracts were planted with eucalyptus, Monterey cypress, and pine, and other areas where buildings and homes are clustered have been planted and landscaped with shrubbery and lawns. Like Golden Gate Park, much of the land was originally covered with sand dunes, but there are outcroppings of serpentine with an interesting association of rare plants still growing wild in these places.

Like an oasis in the desert, this green community attracts a wide variety of birds. Cooper's Hawk and American Kestrel are known to breed here and both Great Horned Owl and Western Screech-Owl are resident. Large flocks of California Quail gather to feed through the underbrush and on the wide lawns. In winter both White-crowned and Golden-crowned Sparrows abound. An occasional White-throated Sparrow has been recorded from these flocks. In spring and early summer the White-crowned Sparrow is one of the most common nesting species, a surprising fact for visiting birders more accustomed to searching out this species in its high mountain breeding habitat. Other common nesting species are the Mourning Dove, Anna's and Allen's Hummingbirds, Chestnut-backed Chickadee, Bushtit, Pygmy Nuthatch, Brown Creeper, Bewick's Wren, American Robin, Hutton's Vireo, Brewer's Blackbird, Purple Finch, House Finch, Pine Siskin, Dark-eyed Junco, and Song Sparrow.

One of the rarest species suspected of nesting on or near the Presidio is the Red Crossbill. It has been recorded at all seasons of the year, often with immature individuals in the small flocks. Perhaps the best areas to search for this bird are around the edges of the golf course and on the slope below the Arguello Street overlook. It has also been seen in the woods between Lincoln Boulevard and Baker Beach on the west side of the Presidio.

More certain are the Hooded Orioles which have been nesting in a small colony near Letterman Hospital for at least the last 18 years. The nests seem to be placed only in the fan-leaf palms here — lovely hanging, purse-shaped nests fastened neatly to the underside of a palm leaf and constructed of the fine, tough fibers pulled by the birds from the leaf edges. Carefully search the row of palms along Presidio Boulevard above and below the inter-

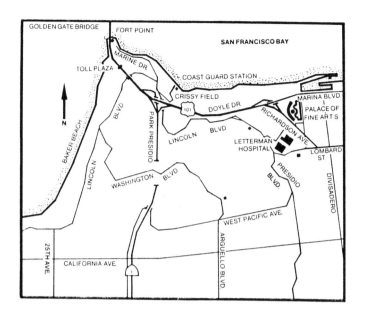

Presidio of San Francisco

section with Lombard Street. There are usually several pairs here and another pair or two near the Girl Scout House and the hospital parking lot near Lombard Gate. There are usually a number of "dummy," or practice, nests in these trees, but quiet, careful watching will reveal the occupied ones. The first birds appear around mid-April with May perhaps the best month to watch their activities. Northern Mockingbirds also nest in this general area.

Occasional Red-breasted Sapsuckers are found here and Northern Flickers and Downy Woodpeckers are fairly common. Large flocks of Cedar Waxwings come and go in winter and spring. Both kinglets, as well as Hermit Thrush, Winter Wren, and Townsend's and Yellow-rumped Warblers are regular winter visitors.

During spring migration almost anything can happen in such an environment. Western Tanagers can be common and so can some of the warblers and vireos. One spring day a Tennessee Warbler announced his presence by singing in the big willow on MacArthur Boulevard, and was then seen by many observers. Ash-throated Flycatcher, Western Bluebird, and Lazuli Bunting, while seldom seen in very large numbers, are regular spring transients.

The fall hawk migration can be spectacular over the Presidio. Most of the species recorded from the Point Diablo hawk lookout at Fort Cronkhite cross over here: Red-tailed Hawks are common and there may be fine accipiter or Osprey days. One of the rarest fall migrants ever recorded on the Presidio was the Clark's Nutcracker. In late October 1961, a group of at least seven birds appeared and spent some days among the pines on Washington Boulevard where it overlooks the ocean (*fide* Naomi Svenningsen).

There is much waterfront on the Presidio — from the baylands on the north side around to Fort Point, under the Golden Gate Bridge and thence to the ocean at Baker Beach. Most productive has been the bay side where loons, grebes, Red-breasted Mergansers, Surf Scoters, and other ducks may be seen close to land. Oldsquaw have been recorded during several winters. Common Murres can often be seen from shore and sometimes Red-necked Phalarope, but lucky are the few who have seen jaegers or skua pursuing gulls or terns from the commissary beach. Forster's Tern can be common and in late summer and fall the Elegant and Common Tern should be watched for. Shorebirds such as Black Turnstone and Sanderling can be common to abundant along the shore here, especially in stormy weather, and the Willet is usually present in small numbers. Most surprising was a Wandering Tattler working the edge of the water on the sandy beach at the Coast Guard Station one late summer day. Recent winters have brought at least one Yellow-billed Loon to the waters below Fort Point and the fishing pier, and large numbers of Northern Fulmars have been visible out across the bay from here. Very rarely, Sooty Shearwaters may come in under the Golden Gate Bridge.

Many species of gull can be studied to advantage around Fort Point and on the old Crissy Field landing strip. This has proven to be a particularly convenient place to see Thayer's Gulls in winter. This is also a good place to study loons and cormorants as they may be quite close, especially around the fishing piers at the Coast Guard Station and at Fort Point. Brown Pelicans are quite common now from about June on through the summer and are usually accompanied by a retinue of Heermann's Gulls. White Pelicans may also appear in small flocks outside the breeding season — always a dramatic sight as they soar by the Golden Gate Bridge and down along the Marina.

So whatever the season, the birder can expect more than the usual excitement of city birding while exploring the Presidio.

Stop first at the Military Police Station for a map if you are unfamiliar with points mentioned above. Most of the area is open to the public, but be sure to respect the off-limits signs and private residences. Good birding.

Directions: There are several entrances to the Presidio; your point of origin may determine the easiest access for you. From the south Bay Area (San Mateo and Santa Clara counties) take Interstate 280 north. The highway becomes 19th Avenue just before the San Francisco city limits, passes through Golden Gate Park, and becomes Park Presidio Boulevard; take the last exit before the Golden Gate Bridge Toll Plaza and head east on Doyle Drive to Lombard Street; turn right at Lombard and Lincoln. From the East Bay, Interstate 80 crosses the Bay Bridge and becomes Highway 101; take the Civic Center-Van Ness Avenue turnoff. Go north on Van Ness several blocks to Lombard Street; turn left onto Lombard and follow it to the Presidio's Lombard Gate. Lombard turns into Lincoln Boulevard here. From Marin County, take the first right exit after passing through the Golden Gate Bridge Toll Plaza. This road goes straight, then veers left past an old gun emplacement. This should put you on Lincoln Boulevard. Near this entrance is a covered Installation Map of the area. Internal maps are available at the Army Museum near the intersection of Lincoln and Funston, as well as at the MP Station.

Facilities: There are restrooms at the Army Museum. Many restaurants and gas stations are located on nearby Lombard Street and in the Richmond District, at the south end of the Presidio.

— Mary Louise Rosegay

Red-breasted Merganser — Cliff Richer

Lake Merced

Lake Merced is probably the single most productive birding area in San Francisco. A variety of habitats and its proximity to the ocean provide an ever-varying avian population. Located in the southwest corner of the city, it attracts large numbers of residents and migrants between September and May. Summer birding tends to be limited to common species, but these include Bank Swallows from the nearby colony at Fort Funston.

North Lake

The Lake Merced Circle (#1), a large parking area at the southern end of Sunset Boulevard, provides excellent birding opportunities. From the circle check the eucalyptus trees to the west for spring and fall migrants as well as Purple Finch and Cedar Waxwings. An American Kestrel can frequently be seen on the wires above the field. The several trails leading to a small fishing beach pass through habitat favored by a number of species of warblers, vireos, sparrows, and hummingbirds. The beach is quiet, and sometimes productive when fishing is prohibited (January-April).

This area has been very productive for rarities during recent winters. Broad-winged Hawk, Summer Tanager, Northern Oriole, and Blue-gray Gnatcatcher have all been observed.

Return to the top of the hill and follow the trail as it circles back to the paved road leading down to the wooden foot bridge (#2). The shoreline in this area should be checked for Green-backed Herons, American Bitterns, Common Moorhen, and assorted waterfowl. As the bridge comes into sight it is worthwhile to check lakeside vegetation for Marsh Wrens, Common Yellowthroats, and Song Sparrows. The silence on the bridge is often broken by the calls of Sora and Virginia Rails in the early mornings and late afternoons. The willows on both sides of the bridge should be checked before returning to the parking lot.

At the top of the hill is Harding Golf Course which has restrooms, a bar, and a restaurant with an excellent view of the lake. A trail to the left follows the fairway along the bank of the lake east to Lake Merced Boulevard. The chances of being hit by a golf ball outweigh the value of birding in this area so it may be best to return across the bridge to the circle.

From the circle walk east until you come to an obscure trail which follows the bank above the lake and parallels the bike path. The willows at the lake's edge provide a winter and spring roost

Lake Merced

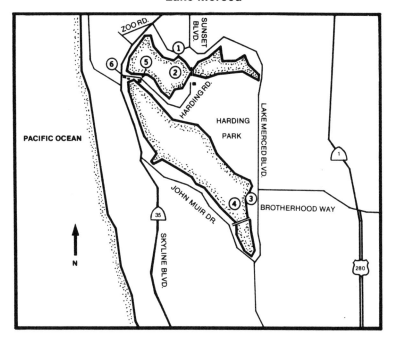

for as many as 70 Black-crowned Night-Herons. Within about a hundred yards the trail drops down to the level of the lake. This is a wonderful place to stop and listen for the calls of Western Grebes and various denizens of the marsh. During early spring mornings you can imagine being far from the city; but by midmorning the illusion is shattered by passing cars, joggers, and dogs.

The hillside to the left generally provides habitat for Anna's Hummingbird, White-crowned Sparrow, Northern Flicker, and Scrub Jay. This area is also productive for mammals including California Ground Squirrel, Brush Rabbit, Oppossum, and even a glimpse of a Long-tailed Weasel may be had.

Continue along the trail as it rises abruptly to the dog running area to the east. A single Loggerhead Shrike sometimes perches on the sign or on small trees. The field, infrequently used by dogs, is the only place in western San Francisco to see Western Meadowlarks with any regularity. As the trail follows the bank be sure to check the shoreline and the willows above it for roosting Black-crowned Night-Herons.

Cross the field to a vantage point next to the eucalyptus grove from which to view the eastern extremity of the lake. Northern

Shoveler, Cinnamon Teal, Greater Scaup, and Canvasback can frequently be seen here in the winter and spring. American Bitterns and Cattle Egrets have been seen in this area as well.

From this point you may continue east to the end of the lake to check the Monterey cypress grove and the willow patch just past it for migrants, or return to the circle by following the bike path west.

South Lake

Drive on Lake Merced Boulevard for 1.7 miles to a small parking area (#3). Below the parking lot is a concrete fishing bridge (#4) which is an excellent place to view Greater Scaup, Horned and Eared Grebes, Mew Gulls, and occasional loons.

During the winters of 1976-1977 and 1977-1978, a Tropical Kingbird stayed here. In the past year a Franklin's Gull and a Red-necked Grebe were seen here as well. A half-mile walk around the southern end of the lake can provide views of large numbers of Ruddy and Ring-necked Ducks in the fall. During other seasons birding is not too productive, but the walk is short and may produce a surprise or two. Pectoral Sandpiper have been seen here as well. Look for all species of swallows, particularly Cliff Swallows which build their mud nests on the side of the bridge. The half-mile walk around the southern end of the lake can be productive. Bufflehead, Ring-necked, and Ruddy Ducks favor the open water. Be sure to check the marsh for Green-backed Herons, Black-crowned Night-Herons and American Bitterns. The fishing pier about 50 yards north of the bridge is certainly worth walking. It passes through a bullrush marsh and provides excellent waterlevel views of many of the previously mentioned birds.

Boathouse

Continue driving around the lake for 2.0 miles to the entrance road marked Lake Merced, Harding Park. Park in the area before reaching the boathouse (#5) on the right. Restrooms, a bar, and a restaurant are located in the building. If you wish to fish or bird from a boat, rentals are available here as well.

The shoreline to the south is frequently used by Great Blue Herons and Black-crowned Night-Herons. Green-backed Herons have been seen here too. The wires in the area are among the first places to find swallows in the late winter and through the spring and summer. Look here for Bank Swallows which frequent the area with the other more common species. Remaining on the south side of the road, walk down toward the piers and follow the path to the right until it ends at a small pump station (#6 on map) beneath the roadside eucalyptus grove. This is the area which has most recently produced rare fall vagrants such as Northern Parula, Northern Waterthrush, Blackpoll Warbler, etc. The beach on the north side of the road should be checked for vagrant shorebirds and waders. Common Moorhens winter here and along the shoreline to the west. Grebes, ducks, and gulls abound here. Thayer's, Mew, Glaucous-winged, Herring, California, and Western Gulls should be seen in the large flock in the middle of the north lake.

By following the road another 1.4 miles you can return to the Lake Merced Circle.

Hiking

For those not interested in driving, perhaps the best hike starts at the circle, crosses the wooden foot bridge, follows the road through Harding Golf Course to the Boathouse area and from there along the bike path back to the circle. This hike is just over two miles in length and passes through much of the most productive birding habitat on the lake. The entire lake may be circled by foot, but birding is not productive along much of the route.

Directions: The lake is at the south end of Sunset Boulevard and at the west end of Brotherhood Way. From the South Bay take Interstate 280 north and either (1) take the Highway 35 (Skyline Boulevard) exit in San Bruno and continue on Highway 35 to Lake Merced, just across the San Mateo County line; or (2) continue on 280 to San Francisco to just after where the freeway splits into Coastal Route 1 and 280; stay on Route 1 for a short distance and head west on Brotherhood Way, to Lake Merced Boulevard. From Marin County, take Route 1 through Golden Gate Park, past San Francisco State University, to Brotherhood Way; turn west on Brotherhood Way to Lake Merced Boulevard. From the east bay, take Highway 101 to the Interstate 280 (Daly City) turnoff; continue on 280 to the John Daly Boulevard exit. Take this exit, turn right, and proceed approximately one mile on John Daly Boulevard; turn right onto Lake Merced Boulevard and follow it to the lake area.

MUNI routes 70 and 72 service the area, as does SamTrans route 21A. From the Daly City BART station it can be reached by taking the MUNI route 91 to Stonestown and walking about a mile west to the lake. Public transportation is changing in this area and it may be worthwhile to check with local transit companies regarding current service.

Facilities: There are restrooms and restaurants in the Harding Park boathouse and the golf course clubhouse.

— Dan Murphy

Other San Francisco Sites

Birders visiting Lake Merced should also see nearby Fort Funston on Highway 35 (Skyline Boulevard). This area is best known for its spring colony of Bank Swallows. The colony is best seen by walking on the beach below Fort Funston's cliffs and looking up at the colony's burrows in the cliff walls. Park cars in one of the lots along Ocean Beach north of Fort Funston and walk south. Scanning the ocean from the top of the cliffs can produce seabirds, including Black Scoters. A variety of land birds can also be found in the area around Fort Funston.

Several groups sponsor boat trips to the Farallon Islands to view breeding birds on the rocks and pelagic birds in flight. The Farallons are 25 miles west of the Golden Gate. Boat parties do not disembark on the ecologically fragile islands but circle them, providing good views of seabirds and marine mammals. Species often seen at or on the way to the islands include Tufted Puffin, Cassin's and Rhinoceros Auklets, Common Murres, Pigeon Guillemots, Arctic Terns, and Northern Fulmar; a variety of shearwaters and jaegers is possible. The Oceanic Society offers weekend day trips cosponsored by the Point Reyes Bird Observatory from June through October; call 415-474-3385. Excursions are occasionally offered through the Golden Gate Audubon Society and the San Francisco Zoological Society (415-661-2023). Policies regarding trips vary among groups.

The Aquatic Park near Ghirardelli Square at the end of Van Ness Avenue has been home to one or more Great-tailed Grackles for the past few years. They stay near the snack stand and are easy to see. Beyond the park, a fishing pier stretches into the bay. From here look for grebes, gulls, mergansers, and pelicans.

Be aware of sounds and movement when passing through any park or open space in San Francisco, especially during migration periods. Vagrants have been drawn to many unexpected spots, seeking shelter as they pass through the city.

NORTH COAST

The North Coast area of San Mateo County provides varied birding just south of San Francisco. The forbidding cliffs of the Devil's Slide area give way to a gentler coastal landscape. There are good birding spots here, both inland and on the coast.

Skyline-Sweeney Ridge Trail

The Sweeney Ridge area lies at the northern end of the San Francisco watershed area between San Bruno and Pacifica. These 1047 acres comprise one eighth of the land mass of the city of Pacifica. Sweeney Ridge became part of the Golden Gate National Recreation Area in February 1984 and was dedicated in a lively public ceremony the following May. As of this writing, GGNRA officials were considering various plans for designating access roads, trails, and facilities in the ridge area.

There are a number of trails leading through the area; however, the Fassler Avenue entrance trail appears to be the trail of choice for many, especially history buffs who wish to follow in the footsteps of Portola.

Starting the trail at the Fassler Avenue entrance, the first three-quarters mile of the road rises steeply and would be described as a moderate to strenuous climb, depending on one's condition. Continue past the water tank on your left, staying to the right at the fork in the road. Stop every now and then to check the skies for Red-tailed Hawks, Turkey Vultures, Sharp-shinned Hawks, Cooper's Hawks, and American Kestrels. Keep your eyes to the skies, as other hawks may be seen along this coastal corridor.

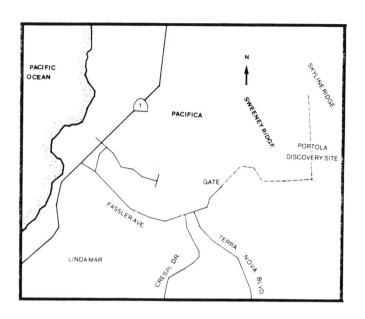

Skyline-Sweeney Ridge Trail

Upon reaching the top, stop to rest and enjoy the beautiful view. Check on top of, in, and around the coyote bushes for White-crowned Sparrows, Fox Sparrows, Wrentits, Song Sparrows, towhees, and Savannah Sparrows. At this point the toughest part of the trail is behind. Wildflowers abound in April. Splashes of bright orange California poppies, pink checker-bloom, blue-eyed grass, blue dicks, mules ears, footsteps-of-springs, sun cups, California buttercups, columbine, Indian paintbrushes, cream cups, and gold fields dot the terrain. Many grasses also cover the coastal hills, along with coyote bush, cow parsnip, ceanothus, poison oak, wax myrtle, soap plant, bee plant, and various thistles.

From the top of the hill, continue in an eastward direction through a small gate in the barbed wire barrier. Listen for the familiar bouncing ball song of the Wrentits. Look for Mourning Doves, blackbirds, Brown-headed Cowbirds, and an occasional Loggerhead Shrike. Western Meadowlarks dot the grasses, and California Quail, hummingbirds, American Robins, American Crows, and swallows are to be found here.

Stay to the left at the power lines, stopping at the rock

outcropping along the road to admire and examine the myriad of small wildflowers, ferns, mosses, lichens, and succulents. Continuing on, a three-way split in the road appears. Take the right fork to the Portola Discovery Site and Skyline Ridge. When you reach the site, spend some time there. You will know the site when you see the monuments erected there to Gaspar de Portola's Expedition of 1769 and the Carl McCarthy Memorial Monument. Portola and his men made the first trip up Sweeney Ridge where they discovered San Francisco Bay 215 years ago. Carl McCarthy was one of those instrumental in founding the Portola Foundation and the driving force in the establishment of the Portola Discovery Site as a historical landmark. Enjoy the spectacular view. The Discovery Site is approximately one and a half miles from Fassler Avenue.

As of this writing, trails and roads are not marked with signs, and when fog shrouds these coastal hills, it is very easy to lose one's bearings. Many trails and roads crisscross. A compass is advisable.

During the spring, there are huge areas of wild iris in bloom, with colors ranging from white through deep purple. Down the road to the south of the Discovery Site along the ridge, watch for Scrub Jays and Northern Mockingbirds. Gulls and ducks fly overhead to and from the Spring Valley Lakes and inland waters. This road follows the ridge approximately three quarters of a mile south to where one encounters the locked Portola Ridge Gate. The property beyond is owned by the San Francisco Water District and special permission must be obtained for extensive access to these lands. There is limited access near the gate.

Backtracking to the Portola Discovery Site, look for deer and rabbits at sunset. From the Discovery Site, retrace your steps to the barbed wire barricade. From this point it is easy to take the wrong road; stay to the left at the fork. The most used trail is not the best one for returning to your car. The entire hike is approximately five miles, and takes about four hours to walk, with stops for snacks, birds, and wildflowers.

Directions: Ten miles south of San Francisco via Coastal Route 1, turn east at the left turn signal in Rockaway Beach, Pacifica, onto Fassler Avenue. Drive to the end of Fassler Avenue and park your car in front of the cyclone fence barricade.

After parking your car at the chain-locked cyclone fence gate, you have the option of climbing over the chain or walking through the side yard of an adjoining residency to gain access to the dirt road that leads to Skyline-Sweeney Ridge.

Facilities: At this writing, there are no facilities in the Sweeney Ridge area itself. Gas stations and restaurants can be found in Pacifica.

Special notes: Permits for access through private properties in the Sweeney Ridge area are available through Pacifica City Hall, Parks, Beach, and Recreation Department; call 415-875-7380 for more information.
Binoculars, bird and flower field guides, food and drink, warm clothes (as the weather changes rapidly), a compass, and good hiking shoes are a must for this area.

— Wanda Belland

San Pedro Valley County Park

San Pedro Valley Park is a beautiful wilderness area located in the foothills of the Santa Cruz Mountain Range in the city of Pacifica. The park's variety of plants and wildlife brings enjoyment to all levels of nature lovers.
The park's trails are very well-marked, and there are good maps available at the Visitor's Center. There are four well-traveled trails in the park: the Old Trout Farm Trail, the Brooks Falls Overlook Trail, Weiler Ranch Road, and the Valley View Trail. These trails abound with plants and wildlife.
The Old Trout Farm Trail brings a variety of birds mainly because it passes through willow bushes and riparian areas along Brooks Creek. This trail is broad and level and is .8 miles long. In the spring and sumer, Swainson's Thrushes, Black-headed Grosbeaks, Northern Orioles, Hutton's Vireos, and Warbling Vireos can be seen. The largest concentration of warblers in the park is found on this trail. Orange-crowned, Yellow, and Wilson's Warblers are common nesting residents. Yellow-rumped, Townsend's, Hermit, and Black-throated Gray Warblers are seen during the spring and fall migration seasons. In late fall and winter, notable species such as Bewick's Wrens, Winter Wrens, Varied Thrushes, Hermit Thrushes, Golden and Ruby-crowned Kinglets, Rufous-sided Towhees, and Fox Sparrows inhabit the Old Trout Farm Trail. Year-round residents include Northern

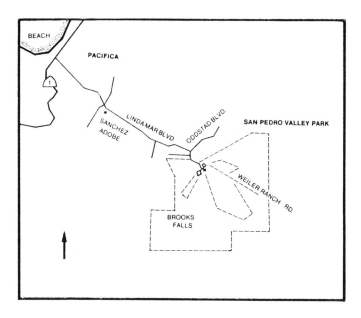

San Pedro Valley County Park

Flicker, Steller's Jay, Chestnut-backed Chickadee, Bushtit, Brown Towhee, Dark-eyed Junco and Song Sparrow. Always keep an eye out for Cooper's and Sharp-shinned Hawks in this area of the park.

The Brooks Falls Overlook Trail starts in the same kind of habitat as does the Old Trout Farm Trail. It then runs up the hillside into brushy areas with scattered young pine and eucalyptus trees. This .7-mile hike is significant because of the beautiful overlook of Brooks Falls, a seasonal waterfall. The falls flow into Brooks Creek, a feeder stream to the south fork of San Pedro Creek, which is tapped annually by the North Coast County Water District to provide 10% of Pacifica's drinking water. In spring and summer, Allen's, Anna's, and sometimes Rufous Hummingbirds can be seen on this trail. Western Flycatchers are especially common during this season of the year. Song Sparrows, Chestnut-backed Chickadees, Downy Woodpeckers, Wrentits, and Bushtits are year-round residents.

The Weiler Ranch Road is the other wide, level trail in the park. This 1.4-mile trail goes through a rather dry area. There are beautiful meadows on the right and grassland hills on the left. At the beginning of the trail, there is the Walnut Grove Group Picnic

Area. In the spring and summer, this area provides excellent habitat for Olive-sided Flycatchers, Purple Finches, House Finches, Pine Siskins, American Goldfinches, and Lesser Goldfinches. In the winter, Dark-eyed Juncos and Fox Sparrows are very fond of this area. Hairy Woodpeckers, Downy Woodpeckers, and Red-breasted Sapsuckers love the walnut trees, and they usually stay year-round. The rest of the Weiler Ranch Road is straight and level. Spring and summer birds expected on this part of the trail include Orange-crowned Warbler, Black-headed Grosbeak, and Western Wood-Pewee. The California Quail, Scrub Jay, Wrentit, Bewick's Wren, Brown Towhee, and Song Sparrow are all year-round residents. California Thrashers are occasionally spotted on this trail. Aerial birds such as Red-tailed Hawks, Turkey Vultures, and American Kestrels can be seen flying overhead. Golden Eagles have been spotted in this area of the park, but no recent records have been recorded.

The Valley View Trail is much like the Weiler Ranch Road, except that it is long, winding, and has some incline. This 1.6-mile hike has about the same species of birds as the Weiler Ranch Road. What this trail has that is different from the Weiler Ranch Road is wildflowers. Many beautiful wildflowers bloom on this trail during the spring. Unfortunately, the trail also has considerable amounts of poison oak. There are many mammals found on the Valley View Trail and the Weiler Ranch Road. Mule Deer, Brush Rabbit, Bobcat, Gray Fox, and Striped Skunk are a few that may be seen in this grassland area.

Directions: Take Coastal Route 1 to the city of Pacifica, which is 10 miles south of San Francisco. Turn east on Linda Mar Boulevard. At its end, turn right on Oddstad Boulevard. Signs will soon direct you into the park.

Facilities: The park has three restroom facilities. Service stations, restaurants, and public telephones are located one block north on Oddstad Boulevard in the Park Mall.

Fee: San Mateo County charges $2.00 to park in the parking lot (1984).

Nearby points of interest: On Linda Mar Boulevard, there is a historical site called the Sanchez Adobe. To view water birds and shorebirds, the nearest beach is San Pedro Beach off Route 1.

Recently, a museum was constructed in the park. It is divided into the five major plant communities that are found in the park.

By using stuffed animals and pressed plants, the displays point out the plants and wildlife of each community.

Publications: There are checklists for birds, mammals, plants, and flowers available in the museum. There are other brochures, but some of them are not specific to the park. The phone number for the park headquarters is 415-355-6489.

Special note: This beautiful park is still undergoing development. New trails are being made that venture further into the wonderful wilderness areas of the California Coastal Mountain Range.

— Scott Smithson

Princeton Harbor — Pillar Point

Princeton Harbor is the only protected harbor on the coast between San Francisco and Santa Cruz. A series of breakwaters running south and east of Pillar Point encloses the harbor, situated at the north end of Half Moon Bay.

Access to the harbor is gained at a number of spots, but the best area for birding is the protected northwest corner, reached as follows: from Coastal Route 1, turn west at the stoplight at Capistrano Road and continue along the north side of the harbor to Prospect Way. Turn left here onto Harvard Avenue and proceed through the boat yards to West Point Avenue, which curves around a small marshy area and heads uphill to the Pillar Point Air Force Station. You must park somewhere along this road near the marsh since the road from this point on is closed to the public. Currently there is a rough, muddy road leading from the paved road to the harbor; however, it is often impossible for cars to navigate and birders are advised to walk the short distance to the harbor.

Be sure to look over the marsh before continuing on. The shallow pond here serves as a stop-over point for small numbers of migrant shorebirds and waterfowl. Uncommon but regular in August and September are Baird's and Pectoral Sandpipers, and Red Phalaropes may be blown into the marsh during windy storms from October to December. Marsh Wrens and Common Yellowthroats are fairly common permanent residents, and winter residents include Sora, Virginia Rail, Black-shouldered Kite, and Lincoln's Sparrow. Tricolored Blackbirds often roost by the

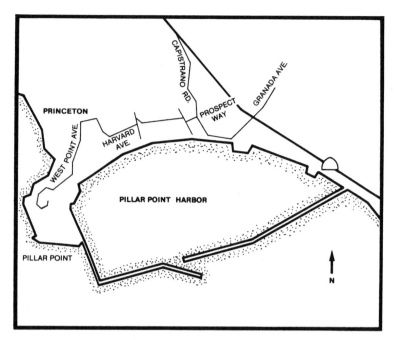

Princeton Harbor — Pillar Point

hundreds in the dense cattails and rushes here, especially during winter months. During most of the day they may be found feeding in freshly cultivated fields in the vicinity of the nearby airport. Common Barn-Owls roost in the willow thickets by day and patrol the surrounding open lands by night. They are resident here and easily heard at night. Although rare, both Long-eared and Short-eared Owls have been seen in the marsh, mainly in winter. The willow thickets are very difficult to enter due to a nearly impenetrable tangle of stinging nettle and blackberry vines; however, birding along the edge or in open areas may be productive. The dense vegetation here, rich in insects, weeds, and cover, attracts migrant songbirds, and many very rare species (most notably eastern warblers) have been observed here, mainly in September and October.

There is a narrow, rough trail which, if not overgrown with weeds, follows the west edge of the marsh from the paved road along the base of the hill toward the sewage facility and trailer park to the north. If you have plenty of time you can walk this trail and birdwatch along the marsh and thicket's edge, then continue past the sewage plant up the hill behind the trailer park to the scrubby ocean bluff above. A few Palm Warblers and Tropical

Kingbirds are seen along this trail each year from October to December. The bluff overlooking the ocean is a good spot in fall and early winter for observing a wide variety of migrants. Several hawks and field birds such as Say's Phoebe, Loggerhead Shrike, and Lincoln's Sparrow are regular here in winter. Continuing south along the bluff toward the Air Force Station you can work your way back toward the harbor.

At the harbor itself, the first stopping point should be the small, sandy beach at the northwest corner. This is a good vantage point to scan the harbor. If the beach is not overrun with people, dogs, and motor vehicles, a flock of one or two dozen Snowy Plovers may be present here, most dependably in fall and winter. Take the dirt trail below the cliffs south along the harbor toward the breakwater, scanning all the while for gulls, terns, scoters, cormorants (Brandt's, Pelagic, Double-crested), loons (Red-throated, Arctic, Common), and grebes (Western, Eared, Horned). Rare but regular and to be checked for are Red-necked Grebe, Black Scoter, Oldsquaw, and Brant. The very rare Yellow-billed Loon has been recorded here on a few occasions. During late summer and fall, schools of small fish often concentrate in the harbor and provide feeding grounds for large numbers of Brown Pelicans, Elegant Terns, and Heermann's Gulls. During this season one or two Parasitic Jaegers may be found near the breakwaters, keeping a watchful eye out for fish-carrying terns. Common Murres and Pigeon Guillemots are common in summer and fall in the vicinity of the harbor and a few Marbled Murrelets are often seen, usually in pairs, further out in the bay. Though of irregular occurrence, small numbers of Ancient Murrelets have been seen here in some winters as well. Other species of alcids (puffins, auklets) occur offshore here and may be identified with a spotting scope if weather conditions and visibility are optimum.

Where the dirt trail reaches the breakwater you will see the rocky Pillar Point reef to the west. During periods of low tide a flat, rocky reef is exposed, rich and diverse in intertidal marine life and consequently quite popular with beachcombers, fishermen, and marine biology students. Several Harbor Seals are usually sunning on the rocks here. During the outgoing and low tides the reef is teeming with feeding shorebirds. American Black Oyster-catcher, Wandering Tattler, Surfbird, Black and Ruddy Turn-stones, Whimbrel, Willet, Marbled Godwit, Black-bellied Plover, and Sanderling are all likely to be seen at all times of the year except perhaps midsummer. A Rock Sandpiper has been present in recent winters, usually in the company of Surfbirds in the rockiest, most tide-washed portions of the reef and breakwaters. Carefully check the gulls which roost on the rocks. In winter, Mew Gulls are very common, Herring Gulls are fairly common, Thayer's Gulls uncommon, and Black-legged Kittiwakes rare. An occasional Glaucous Gull is sighted in winter. Scan the sheer rock cliffs below the Air Force Station in spring and summer for nesting Pelagic Cormorants, Belted Kingfishers, and Northern Rough-winged Swallows.

The tip of Pillar Point is a great vantage point for observing ocean birds, especially if the sea is not rough and one has a good spotting scope and much patience. Sooty Shearwaters may be seen by the thousands from here in late summer and fall, often very close to shore. Artic Loons also may be seen here by the thousands on some days, primarily during spring migration. Northern Fulmars are regular in small numbers during the winter months. Many other pelagic species are possible and even Black-footed Albatross are regularly spotted from here during spring, usually following large ships.

Directions: The harbor is located just west of Coastal Route 1, 18 miles south of San Francisco and 4 miles north of Half Moon Bay. Follow the instructions in the second paragraph to get to the best birding spots.

Facilities: Several new breakwaters are under construction and major tourist-oriented developments (shops, restaurants, etc.) are also underway. Currently there are a few restaurants, fish markets, and even a commercial fishing facility here. Hotels and other facilities are available in nearby Moss Beach and Half Moon Bay.

Nearby points of interest: The Fitzgerald Marine Reserve is located just north of Princeton Harbor in Moss Beach; a sign on Route 1 leads you into the reserve. This is a multiple use area known to scientists as an incredibly rich intertidal region. Its tidepools are habitat for 25 invertebrates discovered here that were new to science, 3 endemic invertebrate species, plus 49 species at the end of their range. There is good birding at the south end of the reserve, near Pillar Point. The reserve is open to the public every day from sunrise to sunset; call 415-728-3584 for more information.

— Peter Metropulos

URBAN CORRIDOR

Much of the bay side of the peninsula from Daly City to Menlo Park is virtually a contiguous corridor of developed areas. Fortunately, there are areas of relief from this urban mass. The Foster City area undoubtedly provides the best birding in this group of sites. This city is bordered by the bay and consists of a series of islands and lagoons, drawing a lively crowd of water-oriented birds, as well as birders of all experience levels.

Aside from Foster City and its environs, the other parks and areas representing the urban corridor are generally small oases for resident and migrating birds. They are probably best suited to novice birdwatchers trying out their skills in familiar territory, or to resident birders studying local species behavior or population dynamics. These are good places to introduce non-birders to the birds found in their own neighborhoods.

Urban Birding — A Few Suggestions

Thousands of birders swarm into the country each week, but relatively few know the joys of urban birding. This type of birdwatching ranges from a vigorous walk around a well-cultivated neighborhood to a visit to a local park to lying quietly in a sunny backyard. Urban birding is valuable to those who can't get to wild areas, providing
- access to nature to the elderly, handicapped, and young;
- a break for working parents who can't leave home for long periods of time;
- an alternative to the businessman's eat and run lunch;

- savings in gas and driving time; and
- freedom from heavy boots or special gear.

Where can you go to bird within city limits? For land birds, head to any area that has trees and landscaped yards — the closer to a natural canyon, the better. Look for water birds in ponds or lagoons; some will even show up in large puddles of water on vacant lots. Many places have been listed in this book that are easily accessible.

About 30 common species can be seen regularly on city streets. Instead of checking off a species and immediately looking for another, take the time to look at behavior. Are they nesting, feeding, courting, or singing? Finding nest sites can be an exciting challenge for the most experienced birder.

Many neighborhood species are associated with certain types of trees. Here are a few suggestions on what to see:

- Deciduous oaks are your best bet, hosting the various titmice, nuthatches, warblers, and woodpeckers.
- Sweet gum trees in winter attract flocks of American and Lesser Goldfinches and Pine Siskins.
- Yellow-rumped Warblers are seen frequently near tall eucalyptus trees.
- House Finches nest frequently in tall Italian cypress trees.
- Look into those large palm trees. Is there a roosting Common Barn-Owl?
- Winter berries attract Northern Mockingbirds, American Robins, and Cedar Waxwings.
- There may be Fox Sparrows, Hermit Thrushes, or Rufous-sided Towhees in your dense shrubbery.

Get to know your neighborhood birds and the complexities of their lives. You'll never say "just a towhee" again!

— Sharon Hom

Sierra Point to Candlestick Point

This area on the shoreline of San Francisco Bay offers views of shorebirds and water birds in winter on the borderline between San Francisco and San Mateo County.

Heading north or south on Highway 101, take the Sierra Point Parkway/Marina Boulevard exit east. From the exit proceed approximately .5 mile on Marina Boulevard to a stop sign (the first stop sign after the road curves north). Turn right at the stop sign

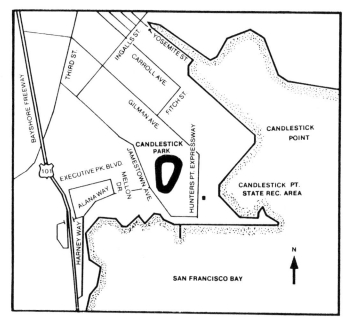

Candlestick Point

and park in one of the nearby parking lots. Walk on the paved path heading north along the marina to the Brisbane Fishing Pier. From this pier you should see diving ducks such as scaup, Canvasbacks, and Ring-necked Ducks, grebes, coots, gulls, Double-crested Cormorants, terns, and Brown Pelicans at various times of the year. Swallows fly above the fields and paved areas in the spring and summer. There are restrooms by the path leading to the pier. There are plans for future development of this area which may include restaurants, office buildings, and landscaped areas.

From Sierra Point birders can retrace their steps and get back on the freeway heading north; proceed two miles to the first Candlestick Point turnoff onto Harney Way and turn left onto Executive Park or one of the other side streets on the left near the large office complex. Walk down to the shoreline. The cove here can provide a variety of shorebirds on good days, including Black-bellied Plovers and Willets, plus often a Great or Snowy Egret. The gravel lot directly above the cove on the bay side is a good place to check for Horned Larks. Return to your car and check the weedy hillside north of the office complex for finches, sparrows, and possibly a Loggerhead Shrike. Scan the skies above here for raptors and White-throated Swifts.

Continue on Harney Way east, following the road around the Candlestick Park complex until you reach the recently opened Candlestick Point State Recreation Area on the east side of the road. This park can yield Western Meadowlarks, Say's Phoebes, Northern Mockingbirds, and House Finches in the grassy areas, Western Sandpipers, Willets, and Snowy Egrets on the shoreline, and ducks, grebes, gulls, and coots in the bay. Burrowing Owls have been seen here on rare occasions.

Die-hard birders may wish to continue on to a small mudflat area in the nearby industrial district that has produced additional species for past San Francisco Bird Blitzes led by the Golden Gate Audubon Society. From the freeway leading around the stadium complex, Harney Way becomes, in turn, Jamestown Avenue, Hunters Point Expressway, and Gilman Avenue. From Gilman Avenue, take a right onto Fitch Street, a left onto Carroll Avenue (passing the brightly painted Candlestick Point SRA building), a right onto Ingalls Street and, three blocks later, a right onto Yosemite Street (not a fitting name by any means) to its dead end. Here you will find a vacant lot full of weeds and thistles, sometimes frequented by American Goldfinches, and beyond the lot is the mudflat. At low tides, the mudflat may be visited by American Avocets, Dunlins, Western and Least Sandpipers, egrets, and a possible variety of other shorebirds. Check wires and roofs of buildings nearby for American Kestrels. You can retrace your steps from here to return to the freeway on days when there are no sporting events at Candlestick Park; otherwise, you should go back to Gilman Avenue, turn right (north) and go several blocks to Third Street. Turn left onto Third Street and follow the directional signs to the freeway.

Directions: Take Highway 101 (Bayshore Freeway) to South San Francisco and the Sierra Point Parkway/Marina Boulevard exit; head east from this exit. Follow directions above in this description to Candlestick Point.

Facilities: There are restrooms and picnic tables at the Candlestick Point State Recreation Area, and restrooms and telephones near the Brisbane Fishing Pier. Restaurants and gas stations can be found in South San Francisco.

Special notes: All of these areas can be cold and windy at times; dress accordingly. Do not attempt to bird the areas near Candlestick Park on any day when a sporting event is taking place unless you have a streak of masochism in your soul. Sports fans driving east on Harney Way to the park on these days drive either direction in all lanes — you will notice at saner times that the lane boundaries are marked for traffic in either direction to facilitate traffic flow before and after events. The Yosemite Avenue mudflat is adjacent to industrial buildings and private property; respect the property lines. Since these areas can be isolated at times, it is best to bird here with a group or a friend.

— Anne Scanlan-Rohrer

Oyster Point

Shorebirds and waterfowl are commonly seen from the shore of San Francisco Bay around Oyster Point in South San Francisco. This heavily developed area was part of the bay until it was filled in in the 1960's to make room for industries and offices. The Oyster Point Marina offers the best bay access, with public parking, picnic tables, and a paved public trail that parallels the shore. Winter is the best time to see most birds, including ducks (Ring-

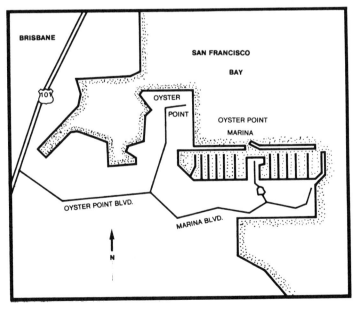

Oyster Point

43

necked Ducks, Greater and Lesser Scaup, Canvasbacks), grebes, gulls, and American White Pelicans. There is a fee to enter the marina area.

Directions: From Highway 101 (Bayshore Freeway) take Oyster Point Boulevard east. Turn right on Marina Boulevard at Oyster Point Marina.

Fee: As of August 1984 there is a $3.00 weekend use fee; eventually this fee will be imposed daily. Marina berth renters do not pay a fee.

Facilities: Public restrooms are available at the end of Marina Boulevard. Nearby is a pier, which was closed to the public as of this writing.

Special notes: Be prepared for strong, cold winds.

— Tom Taber

Sweeney Ridge: San Francisco Watershed Access

Shortly after acquiring the Sweeney Ridge property and assigning it to the Golden Gate National Recreation Area, the federal government sought easements from other governmental bodies in order to provide access to the ridge from the east.

The principal eastern access begins at the end of Sneath Lane in San Bruno. From either El Camino Real or Skyline Boulevard in San Bruno take Sneath Lane to where it ends at a locked gate. As yet, there is no parking lot but there is space for a small number of vehicles on the shoulder of the road. The road is very narrow at this point and may make it extremely difficult for a larger vehicle to be turned around.

The area beyond the gate is part of the San Francisco Watershed and public access was previously prohibited. In late spring of 1984 the prohibition was lifted to the extent of allowing foot traffic along a paved road passing within 100 yards of the Portola memorial at the top of the ridge.

Because of its previous status, this area has no birding history

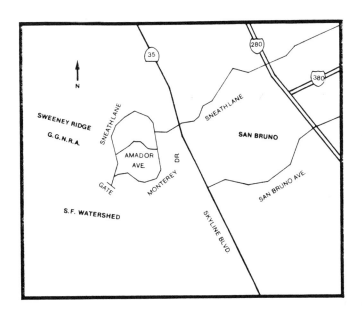

Sweeney Ridge: San Francisco Watershed Access

or documentation but it merits future attention as a good example of relatively undisturbed coastal chaparral habitat. The paved road wends its way at a relatively easy grade approximately 1.5 miles with one moderately steep but short stretch. On a clear day the views of the San Francisco Bay and the peninsula are spectacular, with the panorama stretching from the outskirts of San Jose in the south to Mt. Diablo to the east and are well worth the climb. From the top of the ridge, one can look out over the ocean to the Farallon Islands, Point Reyes, and Mt. Tamalpais to the northwest. A barbed wire fence parallels the road for most of its length, defining the limits of public access, but the density of the chaparral and the presence of poison oak form a more formidable barrier to all but the most dedicated or foolhardy trespasser. The area is managed as a wildlife refuge by the state Department of Fish and Game, and deer, skunks, and raccoons are abundant.

Based on a very few excursions into the area in the summer of 1984; the bird life would seem to be that typical of the coast chaparral. Wrentits, Bushtits, Brown Towhees and White-crowned Sparrows are abundant. Anna's and Allen's Hummingbirds, Red-tailed Hawks, Wilson's Warblers, Bewick's Wrens, Song Sparrows,

Savannah Sparrows, Rufous-sided Towhees, Scrub Jays, Band-tailed Pigeons, American and Lesser Goldfinches, House Finches, Turkey Vultures and California Quail have been identified as nesting species and the absence of starlings, House Sparrows, Brown-headed Cowbirds, and Rock Doves is refreshing. We look forward, over the seasons and years to come, to developing a more comprehensive checklist for this area.

Those who are unfamiliar with our coastal climate should be warned to expect as much as a 20 degree difference in temperature between the sheltered areas near the gate and the ridgetop, particularly when fog is rolling in.

Directions: From El Camino Real (Highway 82) or Skyline Boulevard (Highway 35) in San Bruno, take Sneath Lane west to where it ends at a locked gate.

Facilities: There are none in this part of Sweeney Ridge at this time. There are service stations and restaurants on El Camino Real.

— Cliff Richer

Wrentit — Andrea Hom

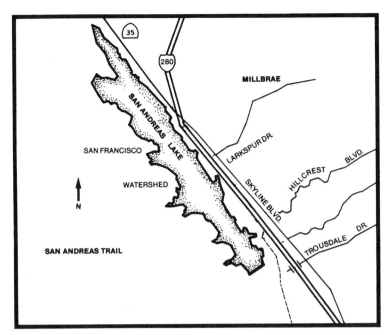

San Andreas Trail

San Andreas Trail

San Andreas Trail follows the eastern boundary of the San Francisco Watershed. The first one and three-quarter miles of trail is paved from the north entrance off Skyline Boulevard in San Bruno until it reaches Larkspur Drive in Millbrae. It then becomes a hiking and equestrian path until it reaches the south entrance at Hillcrest Boulevard in Millbrae. The trail is relatively level and the distance is about three miles one way. The San Andreas Trail connects with the Sawyer Camp Historic Trail to the south.

As you walk down the trail from the north entrance, you can see in the west the point on the ridge from which Gaspar de Portola first saw San Francisco Bay in 1769. You will have lovely views of the San Andreas Lake and the wooded mountains beyond as you walk through groves of Monterey pine and old cypress and open grassy areas. Unfortunately, most of the trail parallels the freeway and the resulting traffic noises intrude on birding by sound.

In spring and fall, migrating Common Loons, Western Grebes, Gadwalls, teal, Common Mergansers, and scaup are almost always seen on the lake. Large flocks of Canada Geese have been seen on the west shores. Red-winged Blackbirds are also in the reeds along the lake. Hawks may be seen perching on the transmission towers along the trail. In winter look for Varied Thrushes, Golden-crowned Kinglets, and crowned sparrows. In late spring and summer, American and Lesser Goldfinches frequent stands of thistle, and terns and swallows skim the lake. In most seasons you should be able to find Pygmy Nuthatch, Acorn Woodpecker, Bewick's Wren, Dark-eyed Junco, House Finch, Purple Finch, and Hermit Thrush.

Directions: South entrance: (a) From Interstate 280 northbound take the Millbrae Avenue exit; go north on the frontage road (Skyline Boulevard) to Hillcrest Boulevard, then west under the freeway and park on Hillcrest Boulevard at the trail entrance. (b) From Interstate 280 southbound take the Larkspur Drive exit, go under the freeway and south on the frontage road to Hillcrest Boulevard where you turn right under the freeway and park at the trail entrance on your right. North entrance: (a) From Interstate 280 northbound take Skyline Boulevard north. The trail entrance is on the west side of the road a short (.1 miles) distance after the divided roadway becomes a two-lane road. (b) From Interstate 280 southbound take the Sneath Lane/San Bruno offramp.

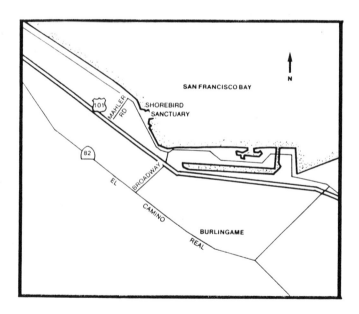

Burlingame Bayfront

Follow the signs south on the frontage road to the signal at San Bruno Boulevard. Turn right onto San Bruno Boulevard and go to the top of the hill to Highway 35 (Skyline Boulevard). Turn left; the park entrance is approximately .45 miles south on the west side of the road.

Facilities: There are no restrooms on the trail. Gas stations are located nearby at the crests of Hillcrest Boulevard and Millbrae Avenue adjacent to Interstate 280. Bring liquids and food with you and dispose of them properly.

— Donna L. Petersen

Burlingame Bayfront

Burlingame's artificial shoreline, located between Millbrae Avenue on the north and Broadway on the south, provides an easy stop for birders. Though this stretch of the bay was filled in the 1960's to make room for office buildings, a few remnants of the once vast salt marshes of the area survive, and mudflats

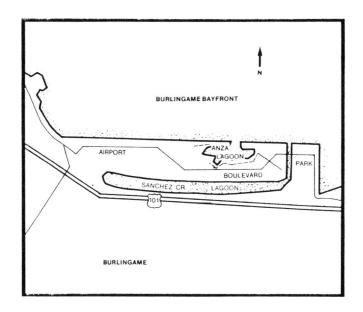

exposed at low tide provide bountiful feeding for shorebirds.

On Bayshore Highway, just south of Mahler Road is a small pocket of saltgrass marsh named the City of Burlingame Shorebird Sanctuary, frequented by herons, egrets, and common shorebirds. Charlie Brown's and Benihana of Tokyo restaurants are on opposite sides of the marsh, both offering landscaped walkways along the bay. With mudflats exposed when the tide is out, you can sit at a window table and watch birds while dining. Forster's Terns hover along the shoreline spring through fall, and several species of gulls and diving ducks float in rafts many yards out at high tide — a spotting scope is necessary for identification.

From the sanctuary, take Bayshore south to Airport Boulevard and turn left. Farther south on Airport Boulevard, take Anza Boulevard to where it ends at the Anza Park Lagoon Public Shore where ducks, coots, and grebes are often seen in the artificial lagoon. A public path continues between the lagoon and the bay, crosses the mouth of the lagoon on a foot bridge and continues south, past Victoria Station restaurant. Scan the bay here with a spotting scope for scoters and other bay ducks. Where Airport Boulevard makes a right angle turn, turn sharply left into Fisherman's Park, the most southern shoreline access in Burlingame. This small park is situated across the cove from Coyote Point. Common Loons, scaup, Western Grebes, and Double-crested Cormorants rest here in the winter.

Burlingame also offers one of the few remaining salt marshes next to Highway 101. Northbound commuters on the freeway may enjoy the sight of Snowy Egrets, Great Egrets, and Great Blue Herons in the marsh just south of the Broadway/Bayshore Highway offramp. In winter, Double-crested Cormorants roost in the transmission towers, and Mallards, Canvasbacks, and scaup are found in the lagoon adjoining the marsh. Shorebirds such as Willets, Killdeer, Black-bellied and Semipalmated Plovers frequent the lagoon's edges. In spring and summer, several species of swallows can be seen chasing insects here, as well as "sea swallows" — terns. Occasionally, a Red-tailed Hawk or Turkey Vulture soars above the eucalyptus trees. Parking is available under this eucalyptus grove, approximately one mile north of the Peninsula Avenue turnoff.

Directions: From northbound Highway 101 in Burlingame, take the Broadway/Bayshore Highway offramp and drive east. Continue straight ahead, past the stoplight, to Airport Boulevard, or turn left at the light to Bayshore Highway. Heading southbound on Highway 101, take the Broadway-Burlingame exit. Stay left following the signs to Old Bayshore Highway/Airport Boulevard and cross the overpass. At the signal turn left onto Bayshore Highway to the Burlingame Shorebird Sanctuary, or turn right at the stop signal and follow the signs to Airport Boulevard.

Facilities: Restrooms are available at restaurants (if you patronize them) and gas stations along Bayshore Highway and Airport Boulevard. A wide variety of cuisines are available at bayshore restaurants. Picnic tables are available at Bayside Park and Fisherman's Park.

Nearby points of interest: The Coyote Point Museum for Environmental Education is also located on the Burlingame shoreline. From the areas mentioned above, follow Airport Boulevard south around the cove and turn left, passing the Peninsula Humane Society on the bay side, until you come to Coyote Point Drive; turn left here, and follow the directional signs for the beach and museum. There is an entrance fee for the Coyote Point Recreational Area. The museum is on top of the eucalyptus-covered hill. The museum features exhibits, dioramas, visual aids, games, and other displays explaining ecological concepts and our relationship to the environment. The museum also supports a Live Animal Center. Call 415-342-7755 for more information on museum schedules and offerings.

Special note: Be prepared for cool and windy weather along the bay.

— Tom Taber

Mills Canyon Park

The beautiful but little known trail in this 28-acre park nestles streamside along Mills Creek between the south boundary of the Mills Estates and just north of the area known as Burlingame Hills. It's a delightful walk, especially in spring and summer, when a green canopy of oak, bay laurel, buckeye, willows, and madrone trees provides a cool cover even on the warmest days. Ferns line

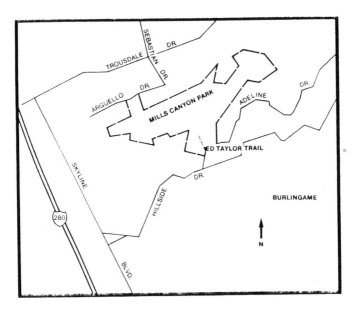

Mills Canyon Park

the stream banks and picturesque moss and lichen-covered rocks add interest to your hike. Spring wildflowers dot the trail as well as the open grassy areas with displays of Douglas iris, blue-eyed grass, buttercups, million bells, mule ears, and Indian paintbrush.

It is a moderately steep up-and-down trail but easily hiked as small steps are cut into the steep parts and small bridges span the wet parts. It is not a true loop trail. When you reach the lowest part of the creek you may either retrace your steps or cross a wooden bridge over the creek to an old paved road on the other side and walk west back to your starting point off Arguello. The birding is, however, best along the creekside trail.

Any spring day you should see and/or hear Wrentit, Downy Woodpecker, Golden-crowned Sparrow, Yellow-rumped, Townsend's, and Wilson's Warblers, Ruby-crowned Kinglet, Rufous-sided Towhee, Western Flycatcher, Hutton's Vireo, Varied Thrush, Hermit Thrush, Chestnut-backed Chickadee, and Bushtit. This is a pleasant walk and good birding any time of the year.

The two-mile Ed Taylor Trail, named for the Burlingame resident who spent many years working on the trail, also winds through the park and can be reached from Adeline Drive near

Hillside Drive in Burlingame. The hike from this entrance is somewhat steeper and more strenuous; the birding is comparable to that found at the Arguello entrance.

Directions: Take Interstate 280 or El Camino Real to Trousdale Drive in Burlingame. Take Trousdale (east from 280, west from El Camino) to Sebastian Drive; turn south. In three blocks, turn right onto Arguello Drive; park where you see yellow posts marking the park entrance. This entrance is opposite a house, #3000 Arguello Drive. The Adeline Drive entrance to the park can be reached by driving south from Trousdale Drive on El Camino Real to Adeline Drive, four blocks from Trousdale Drive. Continue west on Adeline Drive; the street will become narrow and winding. Entrance to the park is across from the house at #2933 Adeline Drive, just before Adeline intersects Hillside Drive.

Facilities: There are no restrooms in the park. Gas stations and restaurants can be found near the intersection of Trousdale Drive and El Camino Real.

Special note: Since both entrances to this park are adjacent to residential areas, do respect the privacy and property of residents at all times.

— Donna L. Petersen

Central Park

This city park in San Mateo provides a variety of year-round backyard birds for the urban birdwatcher. A diverse mixture of trees and plants, including oaks, palms, and conifers, attracts many species, as do the plantings in the Japanese Tea Garden at the northeast end of the park. Many of the native tree species have been labeled with both common and Latin names by the San Mateo Arboretum Society. Visiting the park in the early morning hours is essential, as it becomes crowded later in the day, especially on sunny summer weekends.

Winter is probably the season when park bird species are most numerous. Winter visitors include Yellow-rumped and Townsend's Warblers, Ruby-crowned Kinglets, Hutton's Vireos, and White-crowned and Golden-crowned Sparrows. The trees between the tennis courts and the Japanese Tea Garden are good for warblers. Year-round residents include Acorn and Downy Woodpecker, Northern Flicker, Scrub Jay, Anna's Hummingbirds, Chestnut-backed Chickadee, Mourning Doves, and American Robins. A Red-breasted Sapsucker lived in the Japanese Tea Garden one recent winter, and Belted Kingfishers occasionally dash into the Tea Garden in an attempt to grab a quick meal from the koi carp pond. Visitors who pass through the park at dusk may be rewarded with the chuckling sound overhead of Common Barn-Owls who roost in neighborhood palm trees, or with the sight of small bats (most likely California Myotis) pursuing insects. Fox Squirrels are abundant here.

Directions: The park is located between 5th Avenue, 9th Avenue, Laurel Avenue, and El Camino Real in San Mateo. From Highway 280 or 101 take Highway 92 to the El Camino Real North exit; continue north on El Camino Real nine blocks to 9th Avenue. From Highway 101, you may also take the Third Avenue West exit; take Third to Delaware Street, turn left and proceed south for two blocks, then turn right on Fifth Avenue; the park is a few blocks from this intersection. Parking is available on 5th Avenue and on El Camino Real.

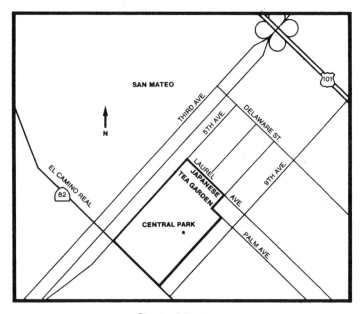

Central Park

Facilities: Central Park is open from dawn to dusk daily. Public restrooms and a snack stand are located in the park itself, and the nearby downtown area has many restaurants and shops. The park also has a playground and miniature train, picnic tables, playing field and tennis courts, and the Central Park Recreation Center, site of many activities for senior citizens.

— Anne Scanlan-Rohrer

Foster City

Foster City is situated at the foot of the San Mateo-Hayward Bridge across San Francisco Bay. It is essentially a group of islands formed as a result of a network of lagoons winding throughout the city. It is surrounded by Marina Lagoon, Belmont Slough, and the San Francisco Bay. Habitat for water birds and shorebirds, including most west coast species, abounds, as well as for marsh and wading birds; this is its chief attraction. Parks, vacant grassy and scrubby areas, plus trees planted throughout the developed areas provide habitat for appropriate species. Raptors patrol much of the shoreline, marshy areas, and fields.

Over 160 species have been observed, including such rarities as the Smew (winters of 1981 through January 1984), Tropical Kingbird, Sage Thrasher, Virginia's Warbler, Eurasian Wigeon, and Tufted Duck. Although rare, Baird's and Pectoral Sandpipers have been seen in spring and fall migration, and Red Knots winter here in fairly large numbers.

The best birding period is September through March, as water-oriented birds winter here by the thousands. Birding during the balance of the year is not too productive. Notable summer residents include several species of swallows and terns. Forster's Terns are common and Caspian and Least Terns occur infrequently. Elegant Terns have occurred in late summer and early fall.

Descriptions of some of the better birding areas follow. Directions are provided; however, the accompanying map should be consulted for better orientation. Please note that some of the areas described here were in a state of alteration or development at the time of this writing.

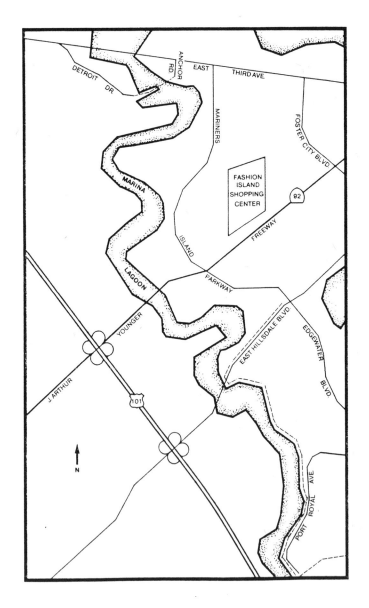

Foster City

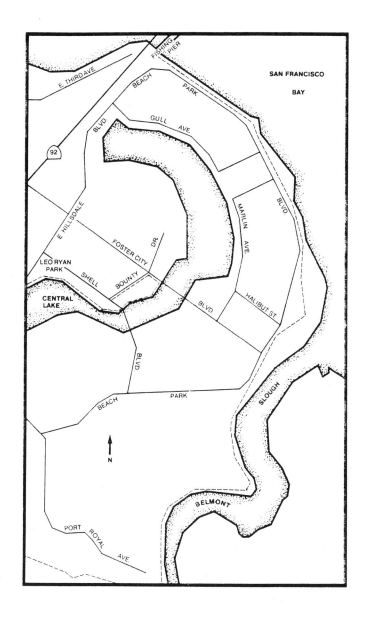

Foster City Lagoons

Much of the lagoon area is not readily accessible, but sufficient areas are available to provide observation of many water-oriented birds. Other species can be seen in adjacent grassy and scrubby fields, bridges, transmission towers, and nearby trees and shrubs.

1. Central Lake

Central Lake is located at Leo Ryan Park, on the south side of Hillsdale Boulevard, between Edgewater and Shell Boulevards. Park along Shell Boulevard just south of the intersection with Hillsdale Boulevard and walk behind the nearby Recreation Center Building or adjacent tennis courts to the lake. Horned Larks are sometimes seen in the grassy area between the building and the tennis courts. The lake is used extensively by boaters and windsurfers, particularly on weekends. Observation is best early to mid-morning and late afternoon.

Wintering birds start arriving in mid to late September, peaking in late November to mid-December, and trailing off in late January through February. Mallards, coots, and diving ducks are usually present in fairly large numbers. Loons, grebes, mergansers, Brown Pelicans, Double-crested Cormorants, Forster's Terns, and various species of gulls are also present.

Rarities have been observed here including a Smew (winters of 1981-1982, 1982-1983, and 1983-1984), Barrow's Goldeneyes, and Red-necked Grebe. A total of 40 Hooded Mergansers were seen here and in nearby lagoons in December 1983.

Restroom facilities are available in the Recreation Center Building as well as in a small building between Hillsdale Boulevard and the lake, just west of Shell Boulevard.

When disbursed from the lake, birds can often be found in the waterways extending from the lake along apartment and condominium buildings. The walkway along the western side of the lagoon is restricted to residents of the apartment complex and is blocked by a fence. However, permission for individuals or very small groups to enter the complex and use the walkway can usually be obtained in the management office of Edgewater Cove Apartments at the corner of Edgewater and Hillsdale Boulevards. Please respect residents' privacy at all times. The walkway can be followed for about a mile to a large arched bridge on Beach Park Boulevard. On the way it will be necessary to go under or around a small, quite low bridge shortly before reaching Beach Park Boulevard. An alternative is to drive south on Edgewater from its intersection with Hillsdale to the Edgewater Place Shopping

Center at the corner of Edgewater and Beach Park Boulevards. Park and walk to the bridge on Beach Park. Many water birds can be observed from both sides of the bridge; however, viewing north back toward Central Lake is usually more rewarding. On several occasions the Smew, Barrow's Goldeneyes, and Hooded Mergansers were observed from the bridge when not present in Central Lake.

The walkway on the eastern side of Central Lake passing the tennis courts can also be followed south for about a mile passing under a bridge on Shell to the bridge on Foster City Boulevard. The Smew has been seen along this walkway very close to shore on several occasions. It is possible to exit at Foster City Boulevard, just before the bridge, walk a short distance north to Bounty Drive, and take it to the left to Shell, where a right turn will take you back to Central Lake. The large open field on the right should be observed for raptors, including Red-tailed Hawk, American Kestrel, Black-shouldered Kite, and Turkey Vultures. Horned Larks, Common Snipe, and Lincoln's Sparrows have been seen in the field. (Unfortunately, this open area has recently been sold and is slated to be developed in the near future.)

When birding along buildings, birders should respect the privacy of residents.

2. Marina Lagoon

Marina Lagoon (also known as Seal Slough) extends from the end of Port Royal Avenue, in a generally northern direction, to an outlet on San Francisco Bay near Third Avenue, a distance of about three miles. Birding the entire length is not practicable; however, some areas can be productive and easy to explore.

The end of Port Royal Avenue can be reached by turning right from Hillsdale Boulevard (when coming from Highway 101) onto Edgewater Boulevard, and proceeding about a mile, passing Edgewater Place Shopping Center, to a right turn on Port Royal Avenue. Drive to the end (about a mile) and walk to the lagoon. At this point water birds, shorebirds, and waders can be found in fall, winter, and spring. In addition to diving ducks, dabbling ducks such as Northern Pintail, wigeons, and Northern Shoveler can be found. Shorebirds usually present include Black-bellied Plover, Killdeer, Greater Yellowlegs, and Spotted Sandpiper. Gulls and Double-crested Cormorants are common. In previous years Hooded Mergansers were frequently seen in the lagoon in fair numbers; however, recently they are more commonly seen in or near Central Lake.

A paved path traverses the lagoon for about two miles, passing under the Hillsdale Boulevard bridge and ending near Edgewater Boulevard at the rear of the Spinnaker Cove condominium complex on Hillsdale Boulevard. Black Phoebe, Loggerhead Shrike, Belted Kingfisher, Yellow-rumped Warbler, and several species of sparrows are usually present beyond the Hillsdale Boulevard bridge in addition to water-oriented birds.

If two or more vehicles are present in a birding group, it is possible to park one at Central Lake (see above discussion on Central Lake) and drive the others to the end of Port Royal Avenue. The lagoon can then be traversed to the end of the paved path. A short walk through a field, often muddy, will lead to Edgewater Boulevard. Walk to the right to Hillsdale Boulevard, then left along Leo Ryan Park to Central Lake. Walking the entire length is only recommended if time permits and if it does not detract from time spent in more productive areas.

Third Avenue Bayshore and Lagoon

Third Avenue extends from San Mateo east to Foster City, and is an exit off the Bayshore Freeway (Highway 101). From Foster City it can be reached by traveling north on Edgewater or Foster City Boulevard.

3. Bayshore

When approaching the bay on East Third Avenue from the Bayshore Freeway, a small dirt turnoff exits to the left .3 miles from the freeway, after crossing Norfolk Street and near Ryder Park. (This area was subject to construction work at the time of writing — there may be construction equipment present.) From a parking area at this turnoff a paved path goes along San Francisco Bay about a mile to Coyote Point. Although outside of Foster City, it can be productive, particularly in the colder months.

Shorebirds and waders, particularly at low tide, plus diving ducks, loons, and mergansers are the chief attraction. Oldsquaw have been seen from the walk and Black Scoters are possible.

San Francisco Bay also borders the north side of Third Avenue starting essentially at the bridge over Marina Lagoon, about a mile east of the Bayshore Freeway exit. The road is currently being widened so construction disruptions plus heavy traffic limit parking near the bridge. Side streets on the right, Detroit Drive and Anchor Road, can be used for parking. At low tide, large concentrations of shorebirds and waders are usually present at

Black-shouldered Kite — Cliff Richer

the mouth of the lagoon, and diving ducks, mergansers, and loons are out on the bay. Raptors are drawn to both the bird concentrations and the rodents and similar prey in nearby marsh and grassy areas. Peregrine Falcons have been observed in winter, plus Red-tailed Hawks, accipiters, and Black-shouldered Kites. Watch for them on the transmission towers in the area.

This area has been under reconstruction during 1984 as the road and bridge are widened. In mitigation for habitat area destroyed by this project, the City of San Mateo is restoring 40 acres in this area to a marsh and wildlife habitat. A portion of this area will be a public park and observation area for wildlife and migratory birds. However, until this restoration project is completed, the status of this area as a birdwatching site will be changing constantly.

An alternate strategy to view Marina Lagoon at this point is to park on Anchor Road off East Third Avenue. On the west side of Anchor Road there is a service vehicle road marked with a sign reading "Service Road Only — No Public Boat Launching." Follow this road to a bridge which crosses the slough. From here the lower end of Marina Lagoon is visible. To view the lagoon mouth, continue walking along this road (which becomes Detroit Drive) toward East Third Avenue.

Further east near Foster City Boulevard, ponds are usually

present from October to April. Shorebirds, waders, and dabbling ducks are usually present. Both Red-necked and Red Phalaropes have been observed here. It is possible to park on Third Avenue near the intersection of Foster City Boulevard; however, it is often better to drive about .4 miles further to the east end of Third Avenue and park. From this point walk to the bayshore levee. Waterfowl should be present in large numbers in winter, particularly Surf, White-winged, and sometimes Black Scoters. Walk along the levee to fully cover the area. Shorebirds are often on the rocks. When possible, depending on how wet it is, walk back to Third Avenue and return along the road. Scan the weedy and wet areas for Lesser Goldfinch, Pine Siskin, and similar species.

Motorcycles use the levee extensively, and can be disruptive when birding this area.

A large open area is located at the east end of Third Avenue between the bay and Highway 92. Burrowing Owls were present here in previous years but have not been seen recently.

4. Lagoon

As mentioned above, a bridge on Third Avenue crosses the Marina Lagoon about one mile east of the Bayshore Freeway. When approaching from that direction turn right on Detroit Drive, just before the bridge, and park as soon as possible. The lagoon mouth can be observed by going around or climbing up a dirt and gravel pile (not very high). This area of the lagoon is different from that mentioned in the above discussion of the bayshore. Shorebirds, wading birds, and other waterfowl are again the chief attraction. Gulls should be numerous. Bonaparte's Gulls have been observed here in late fall. A Belted Kingfisher can often be spotted near the bridge. Look also for raptors on the transmission towers.

After viewing this area, drive to the end of Detroit Drive to view another area of the lagoon where additional water-oriented birds should be present. Raptors, including American Kestrel and Black-shouldered Kites, can often be seen hovering or sitting on poles or wires in the scrubby fields west of Detroit Drive.

5. San Mateo County Fishing Pier

The San Mateo County Fishing Pier offers an excellent opportunity to get a lot closer to many of those bay ducks, grebes, gulls, and cormorants than is possible from shore. An occasional treat is to find Brown Pelicans roosting in the transmission towers or resting in the bay waters.

The pier is one end of the old San Mateo-Hayward Bridge. Approximately 1500 feet long, it is, as its name implies, principally used for fishing these days, but it is also an ideal place for observing the various bay birds. November, December, and January are some of the best months for observing the large number of species which use San Francisco Bay for feeding and resting, including scaup, Canvasbacks, all three scoters, Ruddy Ducks, loons, grebes, and Buffleheads.

If your time is short, the levee which runs along the bay to the south of the Fishing Pier offers a vantage point to look at many of the shorebirds which are resting and feeding in the mudflats at low tide. Look carefully and you might even find a Wandering Tattler among the rocks. Red Knots are often seen among the flocks of Willets, Dunlin, sandpipers, Marbled Godwits, Whimbrels, and Long-billed Curlews which frequent these mudflats. If you have a little more time, an ideal spot to look for shorebirds is approximately one mile south at the oysterbar spit opposite the Beach Park Shopping Center.

Go east on Hillsdale Boulevard from Bayshore Highway (Highway 101) approximately 2.5 miles to the entrance of the San Mateo County Fishing Pier parking lot. This is .2 miles beyond the stop sign at Gull Avenue (the Port of Call Shopping Center is at this intersection) and directly opposite Teal Avenue. The parking lot is open 7 *a.m.* to 6 *p.m.* during the winter months and 7 *a.m.* to 7 *p.m.* in summer.

Belmont Slough

The Belmont Slough extends from San Francisco Bay near the intersection of Halibut Street and Beach Park Boulevard to an area currently occupied by Marine World/Africa USA, a length of about two miles. A paved path along the bay front currently extends along the slough for about a mile where an unsurfaced path goes to its end. There were plans at the time of this writing for it to be extended further by November 1984. An unsurfaced path also extends along the slough on the south side in Redwood Shores. Both sides of the slough provide good birding opportunities and are discussed separately below.

6. Foster City side — Belmont Slough

A marshy area of various widths lies between the above-mentioned path and the slough. A short way along the slough from the bay, near a sign labeled "Belmont Slough Wildlife Area," a path leads to an overlook known as Clapper Rail Point. Clapper

American Avocet — Cliff Richer

Rails are often seen here, particularly at high tides. Great Blue Herons and Black-crowned Night-Herons, as well as Great and Snowy Egrets, are often present, as well as shorebirds and waterfowl. Further along the slough, near a cemented intake, similar birds can be found. Eurasian Wigeons have been present here in winter and Green-winged and Cinnamon Teal are often present in spring. A large flooded pond is situated on the right a short way further along the slough. Many shorebirds, mostly larger species (American Avocet, Black-necked Stilt, Long-billed Curlew, Whimbrel, dowitchers, and Willets), often rest on the small islands in the pond. Several species of gulls and a variety of dabbling ducks, especially wigeon, are also usually present. A walk around the pond, sometimes to see the birds in better light, can be rewarding. While taking this walk, view the lagoon to the west of the pond for more water birds, including grebes, loons, mergansers, and Brown Pelicans.

Water birds predominate in or near the slough as you progress to its end; however, both Canada and White-fronted Geese have been seen on rare occasions. The fields along the path should be scanned for Horned Larks, Water Pipits, sparrows (mostly Savannahs), and Western Meadowlarks. During wet periods, large concentrations of gulls can be seen near flooded spots. Raptors, including American Kestrels, Black-shouldered Kites, Red-tailed Hawks, Northern Harriers, and Turkey Vultures patrol the fields near the slough.

The area to the west of the path, particularly near the flooded pond mentioned above (and perhaps the pond itself) may be altered in the near future, as construction of athletic fields are in the planning stage.

Parking vehicles prior to taking this walk can be a problem as parking is not permitted on Beach Park Boulevard near the slough's juncture with San Francisco Bay. It is recommended that vehicles be parked on side streets (Halibut Street or Cutter Street) as near Beach Park Boulevard as possible. Another possibility is to drive to the end of Port Royal Avenue (see directions in discussion of Marina Lagoon above), park and walk straight ahead to a path to the left which joins the path along the slough. This walk will be in the opposite direction from the one described above. If two or more vehicles are available, one or more could be parked at each end to avoid backtracking.

7. Redwood Shores side — Belmont Slough

To reach the walkway on this side, exit the Bayshore Freeway (Highway 101) at Ralston Avenue, south of Foster City, and take the Marine World Parkway east into Redwood Shores. It is recommended that vehicles be parked off Bridge Parkway where a short walk through a field will take you to the Belmont Slough. The pathway runs to the slough's juncture with San Francisco Bay, then veers to the right along the bay.

Birding on this side of the lagoon is comparable to the Foster City side; however, large flooded areas are present to the right side of the path with a lot of water-oriented birds present. Rails, primarily Clapper Rails, are possible in the marshy areas near the slough. Sparrows, including Song, Savannah, and Lincoln's, can be found along the path and Horned Larks and Water Pipits are in the adjacent fields. Raptors are often seen patrolling the area, particularly Northern Harriers.

Directions: Foster City can be reached by traveling east from the Bayshore Freeway (Highway 101) via the Hillsdale, Highway 92, or Third Avenue exits. From the East Bay it can be reached via the San Mateo-Hayward Bridge (Highway 92) exiting at Foster City Boulevard south.

Facilities: A variety of restaurants are located in Foster City, from short order to large dining rooms. Service stations are present on the main streets. Several shopping centers can also be found with grocery stores, drugstores, and specialty shops. The large Hillsdale Mall is located in San Mateo about a mile west of Foster City via Hillsdale Boulevard and the large Fashion Island Shopping Center is located to the north via Edgewater Boulevard. Both include large department stores, specialty shops, and restaurants.

Nearby points of interest: See the Redwood Shores description following in this section.

Publications: The Sequoia Audubon Society has a checklist of the birds of Foster City; contact the chapter office for details.

Special note: A spotting scope is very helpful when birding most areas of Foster City.

— Nick Coiro

Redwood Shores

Redwood Shores is the residential area on the bay in Redwood City, near Belmont. The development is relatively recent and several undeveloped areas exist, providing habitat for a variety of water-oriented birds.

Belmont Channel, on the northwest side of Redwood Shores, is a good spot to get close views of common wintering waterfowl. Ducks often seen are Common Goldeneyes, Buffleheads, Ruddy

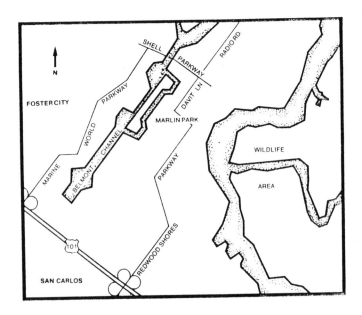

Redwood Shores

Ducks, Canvasbacks, Northern Pintails, scaups, scoters, and Mallards. Egrets stand on the banks waiting for small fish. The large herds of gray birds grazing on the playing fields in nearby Marlin Park are American Coots. In mid-winter, shorebirds often feed or stand in rainwater puddles on shore. Grebes and cormorants come to this quiet channel to rest and feed. In summer, families of Mallards bob on the water close to shore. Look for Caspian or Forster's Terns plunging to the surface for fish. During the warm months, the best time to visit is in the morning, to avoid the crowds using Marlin Park, a residential park bordered on one side by Belmont Channel.

The Radio Road end of Belmont Channel is a currently undeveloped area. The road goes by a series of channels and ponds. Look at all the ponds; each has a different assemblage of ducks and shorebirds. At the end of the road is a large rainwater pond, a good place to see dabbling ducks and flocks of resting shorebirds during high tide. In summer, there are pelicans and terns here, including possibly a rare Least Tern coming from nearby Bair Island.

Directions: Take Highway 101 to the Holly Street exit in San Carlos and continue east towards the bay on Redwood Shores Parkway. Turn left on Marlin Drive and park at the corner of Davit and Marlin. Walk to your left along the dirt path to the lagoon. This is Marlin Park. To reach the Radio Road section of Belmont Channel, continue along Davit Lane and cross Shell Parkway. Radio Road is about a mile long and dead-ends at the sewage treatment plant. This is a restricted area! You may drive or stand on the road, but do not go into the surrounding areas.

Facilities: Restrooms are available at the Marlin Park picnic area. For gas stations and restaurants, take Holly Street west over Highway 101 to El Camino Real.

Special notes: This area allows you to combine birding with other recreation. Marlin Park has soccer fields, a playground, a picnic area, and a parcourse available. This area is recommended for senior citizens and groups of children. For the wheelchair-bound, the lagoon continues along Davit Lane with a sidewalk paralleling it.

— Sharon Hom

Bair Island

Bair Island was formerly the collective name for what is actually a complex of three islands separated by sloughs near Redwood Shores. The complex is now known as South Shores, and Bair Island is used to mean only the outer island. This isolated area provides habitat for an abundance of wildlife and plants, drawn by the island's relative freedom from intrusion by people and domestic animals. The area was in the center of a controversy in 1982 when South Shores Inc. (a division of Mobil Oil), owner of the land on the inner and middle islands, had plans for residential, commercial, and industrial development on their property. The plans were halted by a Redwood City referendum vote. The future of the island complex regarding development is uncertain.

Part of the land on the outer island is under the jurisdiction of the San Francisco Bay National Wildlife Refuge, and access for visitors is strictly limited and varies depending on the season and wildlife activity in the area. Nature Explorations of Palo Alto (415-324-8737) has offered a limited number of trips to the outer island during past spring seasons.

Residents of the island complex include California Clapper Rail, Northern Harrier, Short-eared Owl, Black-shouldered Kite, and numerous shorebirds and waterfowl. There are breeding colonies of Snowy Egrets, Great Blue Herons, and Black-crowned Night-Herons flourishing on the island. In past years, the island supported a colony of California Least Terns and the largest West Coast colony of Caspian Terns. In 1984, the numbers of both tern species dropped dramatically. It is possible that the presence of people building a new levee for Least Tern breeding colonies disturbed the terns, but the reason is uncertain. In the same year, the breeding pairs of Black-crowned Night-Herons, Snowy Egrets, and Black-shouldered Kites were very successful in raising young. It is because the area is subject to such natural fluctuations that it is restricted in use. The people at the San Francisco Bay Bird Observatory (408-946-6548) are happy to answer questions about Bair Island.

Although access for birding the island is severely limited, the ecological importance of Bair Island necessitates its mention.

— Anne Scanlan-Rohrer

Waterdog Lake and Sheep Camp Trail

This area in the hills of Belmont provides an enjoyable hike through oaks, chaparral, and grasslands, providing views of all of the common species of these habitats. From the lower trail entrance on Lyall, Waterdog Lake lies about three-quarters of a mile away. Look for goldfinches feeding on thistles in the grassy areas. Flocks of Bushtits and chickadees regularly visit trees along the trail. Warblers often join these flocks, so watch them carefully.

Waterdog Lake is too popular with people to be a breeding ground for water birds, but the occasional duck or egret uses the lake as a stop over. You may walk from the end of the dam to the

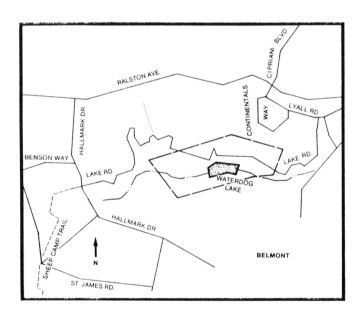

Waterdog Lake and Sheep Camp Trail

cattails, where Red-winged Blackbirds nest in the spring. Black Phoebes and warblers are often found lurking in the cattails and willows. The trail is narrow and steep, so watch your step. On the trail above the lake, look for Blue-gray Gnatcatchers and Orange-crowned Warblers in the spring. Wrentits and Bewick's Wrens are frequently found in brushy areas. The trail ends after a total of two miles at Hallmark Drive. Cross the street and find the narrower trail behind the utility station. This section continues for about a half mile behind houses and through oaks, and emerges at St. James Road. Across the street is Sheep Camp Trail, which meanders for one and a half miles through the watershed before it crosses Interstate 280 and ends on Canada Road.

The first part of the trail descends the hill through grassland. This is a good place to see flocks of Western Meadowlarks singing in the morning. West of Interstate 280, look overhead for raptors, especially Black-shouldered Kites and Northern Harriers. California Thrashers, Wrentits, and Bewick's Wrens are frequent in the large teazle and coyote brush area just west of the freeway.

Directions: (1) Waterdog Lake, upper entrance. From Interstate 280 go east on Highway 92 to Ralston Avenue. Turn right onto Hallmark Drive. The trailhead begins at the intersection with Lake Road, .1 mile down Hallmark. (2) Waterdog Lake, lower entrance. From Highway 101 take the Ralston Avenue exit west for approximately two miles to Lyall Road, which is the first street on the left west of Alameda de las Pulgas. Turn left onto Lyall and follow it to Lake Road. Park near the intersection of Lake and Lyall. Waterdog Lake Trail starts at an inset gate at the intersection. (3) Sheep Camp Trail. From Ralston Avenue turn onto Hallmark Drive. Turn right at Benson Way, then left again at St. James Road. The trailhead is about a quarter of a mile down St. James on the right side.

Special notes: Runners can exercise on the cross-country trail ·that starts at the Sheep Camp Trail entrance on St. James Road. Waterdog Lake is a popular fishing hole. Swimming has been banned since an accidental drowning. The trail is wide and unpaved but fairly smooth; it is not accessible to wheelchairs, but easy enough for slow walkers. SamTrans buses run past the Lyall (route 40E), Hallmark, and St. James entrances (route 45B). Call the SamTrans office for current information and schedules.

— Sharon Hom

SOUTH COUNTY PARKS

The southern end of San Mateo County is marked by a number of parks and open space areas. Many of these are in the coast range of mountains and exhibit a redwood/mixed forest habitat, as in Huddart and Wunderlich Parks. The other notable type of park found in the south county is the grassland/oak woodland habitat, exemplified by Edgewood County Park and Jasper Ridge Biological Preserve.

This section describes areas representing a cross-section of the south county parks and is by no means intended to be all-inclusive. The habitat and bird species found in each of the redwood parks are similar enough that describing each in detail would be somewhat redundant. The park areas are also limited for birding at certain times of the year; summer weekends draw large numbers of group picnickers, causing wildlife to go into seclusion at these times. Secluded trails in these parks are the best bet for birding at this time.

However, individual birders may prefer exploring south county parks other than those described here. Other parks in this area include Butano State Park, Pescadero Creek County Park, Portola State Park, Sam McDonald Park, San Mateo County Memorial Park, and Windy Hill Open Space Preserve.

Edgewood County Park

Close to the urban areas of San Mateo County exists the 467-acre Edgewood County Park which contains a rich sampling of three major habitats: oak woodland, chaparral, and grassland.

White-breasted Nuthatch — Andrea Hom

Within each of these habitats or ecological niches can be found certain animals and plants that have found their most favorable place for survival. As the park is on the edge of the continental flyway, approximately 70 species of birds are found here, including migrants and residents. The greatest number of species (45-60) at varying seasons can be found in the oak woodland habitat; 20-30 species can be found in the other major habitats.

Because some birds are specialized feeders they can only be found in certain areas, while others frequent many or all of the habitats. Eucalyptus trees found in two areas attract many songbirds, as do the remnants of an olive grove. As food resources for birds, over 300 species of plants have been identified within the park. Of interest to botanists are a variety of rare plants: San Mateo thornmint, Marin dwarf flax, San Francisco campion, fragrant fritillaria, San Francisco collinsia, white-rayed pentachaeta, and ruddy clarkia. The park contains 110 acres of serpentine soil which support a grassland rich in native and endemic species. Water sources include minor wetlands with permanent springs and seeps. Seasonal runoffs provide streams in the winter and spring.

Recognizing the plant life in an area can be a means of anticipating the birds to be expected and/or identified. Indicators of species can be criteria such as which birds are seekers of seeds, fruits, nectar, sap, and/or insects from certain plants, as well as what trees are used for nesting and storage and what parts of plants are used to build nests.

As an introduction to birding in this area, it is recommended that birders follow the approximately two-mile trail around the ridge in the park's center that stands out like a tree-capped island with its shores buried in waves of grasslands. The habitat found on the ridge is primarily oak woodland on the north side and top, and chaparral on the south side. The views of San Francisco Bay and Crystal Springs Lake from the trails are spectacular. With few exceptions, all of the new trails have a 10% gradient. Avoid using trails made by motorcycles and off-road vehicles, since these areas are being reseeded currently. Don't add to erosion!

Below is a partial plant list of flora found on the ridge:
Trees: madrone, white oak, live oak, Garry's oak, scrub oak, buckeye, bay laurel
Understory: poison oak (!!), coffee berry, honeysuckle, toyon, bedstraw
Chaparral: chamise, coyote brush, chaparral pea, snowberry, monkey flower, pitcher sage, ceanothus, buck brush, California broom
Grasses: brome grass ssp., stipa ssp., oat grass, squirreltail quaking grass
Other: ferns, lichens, mosses, fungi
Viewed from the ridge from March to May, the grasslands below provide an annual display of spring flowers of exceptional beauty.

Following is a list of bird species found in the park.

Code: **Habitat:** A=Aerial/G=Grassland/C=Chaparral/W=Oak-Woodland
Season: Wi=Winter/Sp=Spring/Su=Summer/Fa=Fall/Yr=Year around.

Vulture, Turkey A @ Sp-Fa
Kite, Black-shouldered A,G @ Fa,Wi
Hawk, Sharp-shinned A,W @ Fa,Wi,Sp
    Cooper's A,W @ Fa,Wi,Sp
    Red-tailed A,W @ Yr
    Red-shouldered A @ Yr
Harrier, Northern A @ Fa,Wi
Kestrel, American A @ Yr
Eagle, Golden A @ Yr
Quail, California G,W,C @ Yr
Pigeon, Band-tailed W @ Yr
Dove, Mourning G,W @ Yr
    Rock A,W @ Yr
Owl, Great Horned W @ Yr
    Burrowing G @ Yr
Hummingbird, Anna's W,C @ Yr
    Allen's W,C @ Yr
Flicker, Northern W @ Yr
Woodpecker, Hairy W @ Yr
    Downy W @ Yr
    Nuttall's W @ Rare
Flycatcher, Ash-throated W @ Sp,Su,Fa
Phoebe, Black C @ Yr
    Say's G @ Fa,Wi,Sp
Pewee, Western Wood W @ Sp,Su
Swallows, Violet-green A @ Sp,Su
    Rough-winged A @ Sp,Su
    Barn A @ Sp-Su
    Cliff A @ Sp,Su
Jay, Scrub W,C @ Yr
    Steller's W @ Yr
Raven, Common A @ Wi,Fa
Crow, American A @ Yr
Chickadee, Chestnut-backed W @ Yr
Titmouse, Plain W @ Yr
Bushtit W, C @ Yr
Nuthatch, White-breasted W @ Sp,Su
Creeper, Brown W @ Yr

Wrentit W,C @Yr
Wren, Bewick's W,C, @ Yr
Mockingbird, Northern G,W, @ Yr
Thrasher, California W,C @ Yr
Robin, American W @ Yr
Thrush, Hermit W,C @ Yr
    Varied W @ Fa,Wi
    Swainson's W @ Sp,Su
Bluebird, Western G,W @ Yr
Gnatcatcher, Blue-gray W,C @ Su
Kinglet, Ruby-crowned W @ Fa,Wi,Sp
    Golden-crowned W @ Fa,Wi
Starling, European W @ Yr
Vireo, Hutton's W @ Yr
Warbler, Orange-crowned W,C @ Sp,Su
    Yellow-rumped W @ Yr
    Townsend's W @ Fa,Wi,Sp
    Wilson's W @ Sp, Su,Fa
Meadowlark, Western G @ Yr
Blackbird, Brewer's G,W @ Yr
Oriole, Northern W @ Sp,Su
Grosbeak, Black-headed W @ Sp,Su,Fa
Finch, Purple W @ Yr
Sparrow, House G,W,C, @ Yr
Pine Siskin G,W @ Yr
Goldfinch, American G,C, @ Yr
    Lesser W,C @ Yr
Towhee, Brown W,C @ Yr
    Rufous-sided W,C @ Yr
Junco, Dark-eyed W,C @ Yr
Sparrow, White-crowned G,W,C @ Yr
    Golden-crowned W,C @ Yr
    Fox W,C @ Fa,Wi
    Lark G @ Yr
    Song G @ Yr
    Chipping W @ Sp,Su
    Savannah G @ Yr

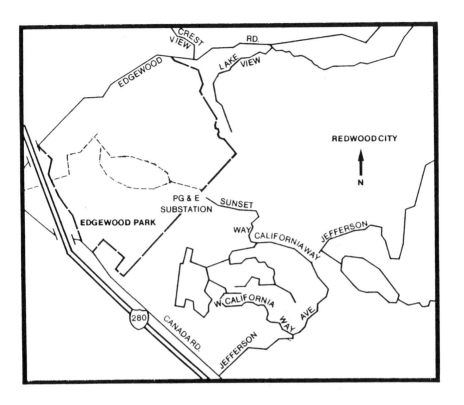

Edgewood County Park

Directions: There are three entrances to the park: Sunset Way, Edgewood Road west of Interstate 280, and south side of Edgewood Road adjacent to Crestview Drive. The best entrance to the ridge trail is at the junction of Sunset Way and Hillcrest Way. Take Jefferson Avenue west from El Camino Real (Highway 82) in Redwood City (aim for the cross on the hill). Turn right on California Way (firehouse on the corner). Park at the junction of Sunset Way and Hillcrest Way. Walk past the PG&E substation to the locked service road gate. The entrance is adjacent to the gate. Follow the service road to the right, where San Francisco Bay can be seen. The trail starts on the left.

Facilities: There are no restrooms or any other kind of facilities at Edgewood County Park. San Mateo County has plans for future development of this area which may include restrooms, day camp areas, and a golf course.

Publications: Those interested in the relationship of plants and birds as an aid to identification may wish to read *American Wildlife and Plants (A Guide to Wildlife Food Habits)* by Martin, Zim, and Nelson (Dover Paperback), or the section on food and feeding habits in the *Audubon Society Encyclopedia of North American Birds* by John K. Terres (Alfred A. Knopf). Recommended publications on plants of the area are *Native Shrubs of the San Francisco Bay Region* by Roxanna Ferris and *Native Trees of the San Francisco Bay Region* by Woodbridge Metcalf (both University of California Press paperbacks).

— Wilma Rockman

Huddart County Park

Huddart County Park is one of San Mateo County's most versatile recreation areas. The 973 acres offer the opportunity to bird in redwood/Douglas fir forest, oak woodland, madrone, and California bay laurel associations, as well as creekside and riparian habitats. Bird life is plentiful and diverse. Species commonly seen include Red-tailed Hawks, California Quail, Hairy and Downy Woodpeckers, Red-breasted Sapsuckers, nuthatches, Brown Creepers, Bewick's Wren, Swainson's and Varied Thrushes, California Thrasher, and the usual complement of hummingbirds, titmice, chickadees, juncos, and Wrentits.

The park is open year-round from dawn to dusk. Birding in the fall and winter when park use is light can be rewarding. Huddart Park has an extensive hiking trail system, group and individual picnic areas, equestrian trails, and even an archery range. There is a trailhead off Kings Mountain Road west of the main entrance, and another trailhead north of the intersection of Kings Mountain Road and Skyline Boulevard on Skyline. Be sure to park without blocking driveways, and watch for "no parking anytime" signs. There is also a trail through the California Water Company — Bear Gulch Watershed paralleling Skyline Boulevard, which connects Huddart Park with Wunderlich Park. As of 1984,

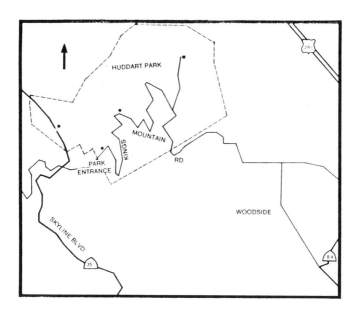

Huddart County Park

Huddart Park's Master Plan had just been revised and improvements of the facilities have begun. Some trails will be realigned; however, impact will be mainly on upgrading recreational facilities.

Directions: Huddart County Park's main entrance is off Kings Mountain Road in Woodside. From Interstate 280 exit at Woodside Road West (Highway 84) and proceed west for approximately 1.5 miles. Veer right onto Kings Mountain Road and follow it along for two miles (the road winds considerably) to the main entrance on your right.

Facilities: There are restroom facilities and running water; consult maps available at the park entrance for exact locations of facilities and trails.

Fee: There is a $2.00 entrance fee per car as of 1984; reservations are needed in advance for the group picnic grounds.

— Donna Kirsacko

Wunderlich Park

A 1974 gift of 942 acres of coniferous forest and meadows provided birders with Wunderlich Park, an exciting wildlife area.

Between 1850 and 1870 all the large redwoods in this area were cut to build San Francisco. The lumber was hauled to the bay in Redwood City and sailed by schooner to San Francisco. The lowlands around Wunderlich Park were farmed, while the hillside forests have acquired a second growth. James A. Folger, the second owner of the farmed lands, named Hazelwood Farm for the hazelnut shrubs in the forest, built the handsome stable across from the parking lot in early 1900. An application has been made to register the stable as a historic building, and ways are being sought to finance needed restorations. Martin Wunderlich, the third owner, acquired much of the Folger estate in 1956 and in 1974 generously gave 942 acres to San Mateo County for open space and park use. Today, the county has completed 25 miles of trails, and it is possible to walk the 10 miles from Skyline Boulevard down to the park or several shorter loops.

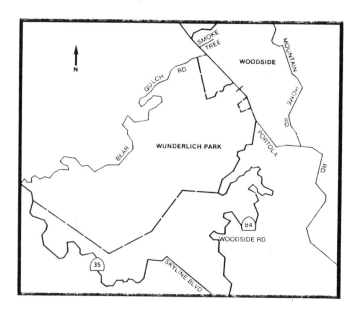

Wunderlich Park

The park is open year-round from 8 *a.m.* until dusk, and there is usually a park ranger on duty. Birding is best in the springtime. When birding at Wunderlich, be sure to step aside for equestrians and don't startle the horses. The many trails are described in detail in the book *Peninsula Trails* by Jean Rusmore and Frances Spangle.

Connecting trails make it possible to walk loops from one to ten miles through mixed woodlands of black oaks, toyons, canyon oaks, and madrones, which may yield the following bird species: Turkey Vulture, Red-tailed and Red-shouldered Hawks, Golden Eagle, California Quail, Band-tailed Pigeon, Mourning Dove, Anna's, Rufous, and Allen's Hummingbirds, Northern Flicker, Acorn, Downy, and Hairy Woodpecker, Red-breasted Sapsucker, Steller's and Scrub Jay, Chestnut-backed Chickadee, Plain Titmouse, Bushtit, White-breasted and Pygmy Nuthatches, Brown Creeper, Wrentit, Bewick's Wren, California Thrasher, American Robin, Hermit and Varied Thrushes, Ruby-crowned Kinglet, European Starling, Hutton's and Warbling Vireos, Orange-crowned, Yellow-rumped, and Townsend's Warblers, Purple Finch, Rufous-sided and Brown Towhees, Dark-eyed Junco, and Golden-crowned Sparrow.

In the spring, Douglas iris, poppies, sword fern, gold-back fern, woodwardia, and giant chain fern decorate the trails. Baby blue eyes, lupines, hound's tongue, milkmaids, Indian warrior, sticky monkey flower, hazelnut, buckeye, and gooseberry also thrive in the shady forest. Other native plants may be seen in the well-kept Native Plant Garden behind the Woodside Library on Woodside Road near town.

Directions: Take Interstate 280 to the Highway 84 (Woodside Road) exit and turn west. From the town of Woodside after Woodside Road, Highway 84 turns south; look for Bear Gulch Road. About one-quarter mile past it you will see the small park sign on the right. This is 1.7 miles from the Woodside Town Hall.

Facilities: There are portable toilets at the parking lot for Wunderlich Park. Gas stations and restaurants can be found in the nearby towns of Woodside and Portola Valley.

Publications: As mentioned above, *Peninsula Trails* by Rusmore and Spangle has detailed trail maps for Wunderlich Park.

— Jean and Frank Allen

Skyline Ridge Open Space Preserve

Skyline Ridge Open Space Preserve is a 944-acre preserve adjacent to the intersection of Skyline Boulevard, Page Mill, and Alpine Roads. It is part of the Skyline Scenic Corridor within the Santa Cruz Mountains, and is owned by the Midpeninsula Regional Open Space District (MROSD). Visitors to the preserve can look down from one of its many high points to view a wilderness area comprised of chaparral, coastal scrub, grasslands, small lakes, and mixed evergreen forest. The forest is dominated by canyon live oak, and also includes California bay laurel, bigleaf maple, madrone, and tan oak.

The variety of habitats appear to attract an equally diverse bird population. Since the preserve has been open to the public for a relatively short time, there have proportionately been a limited number of birding trips to this area, but these few excursions have been very promising. Entering the preserve at the Alpine Road entrance, you are immediately greeted by the calls of California Quail, Acorn Woodpeckers, Northern Flicker, White-breasted Nuthatches, and Steller's Jays. Walk on the dirt path around the north edge of Alpine Lake to see Violet-green and Barn Swallows dashing over the lake. Take the paved path bordering the lake east to the grassland and scrub areas to find Lesser Goldfinches feeding on thistles, or take the same path west through the forest for Downy Woodpeckers, Hutton's Vireos, and Bewick's Wrens. Flocks of Band-tailed Pigeons fly overhead frequently.

During summer of 1984, 40 to 50 species were easily found here on just a few trips to the preserve. Birds seen at that time included Red-breasted Nuthatch, Western Tanager, Lazuli Bunting, Lark and Chipping Sparrows, Red Crossbills, and Yellow-rumped Warblers with young. A Calliope Hummingbird seen here was a record sighting for San Mateo County.

Part of the land on the preserve was a Christmas tree farm for many years. Former owners of the land still live on the preserve through a 50-year lease with MROSD. Other buildings evident on the preserve may be used for recreational purposes. MROSD is currently working with the Peninsula Open Space Trust (POST) on a master plan for the preserve. The major objective of the plan is to provide recreational facilities while maintaining the wild and fragile nature of the land. POST and MROSD encourage public input regarding the preserve; for information regarding hearings on the preserve, call POST at 415-854-7696 or MROSD at 415-

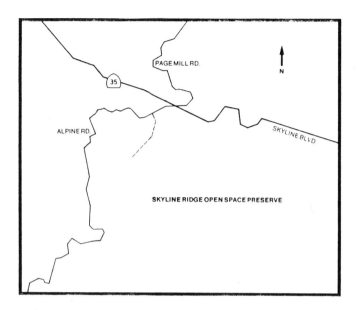

Skyline Ridge Open Space Preserve

965-4717. Possible developments may include improved access and parking areas, trail loops for hikers, cyclists, and equestrians, an interpretive center, picnic and camping facilities, fishing access, a meeting center, a youth hostel, ranger facilities, and emergency service facilities.

Skyline Ridge Open Space Preserve is a beautiful area and a very welcome addition to the county's greenbelt, and has great potential as a prime birding spot.

Directions: From Highway 101 or Interstate 280 take Highway 84 (Woodside ·Road) west through the town of Woodside to the intersection of Highway 84 with Skyline Boulevard (Highway 35). Take Skyline south approximately seven miles to its intersection with Page Mill and Alpine Roads. Turn right (west) onto Alpine Road and park immediately on the right side of the road near the "Narrow Road Next 3 Miles" sign. The preserve entrance is across the road from this sign. There is additional parking along the other sides of this intersection. Another entrance to the preserve is on Skyline Boulevard one mile south of Alpine Road, near the "Horse Crossing" sign. Park on Skyline near this sign. There is access to the land on either side of the road. This part of the preserve has been known as Skyline Ranch Christmas Tree Farm.

Facilities: There are no facilities at this time. Service stations and restaurants can be found at the intersection of Skyline Boulevard and Highway 84, and in the town of Woodside.

Nearby points of interest: Following Alpine Road further west will take you to Portola State Park and, eventually, Sam McDonald County Park, Pescadero Creek County Park, and San Mateo County Memorial Park. Heading west, Highway 84 passes through Woodside and leads past the entrance roads to both Huddart County Park and Wunderlich Park (see descriptions of these two parks in this section).

— Frank and Jean Allen
Anne Scanlan-Rohrer

Jasper Ridge Biological Preserve

Jasper Ridge is Stanford University's Biological Preserve. Its 1300 acres contain samplings of every terrestrial habitat of the peninsula. There is a correspondingly diverse bird species list: 142 regularly occurring and nearly 30 casuals and accidentals. Guided tours are available year-round (see Directions).

Searsville Lake was a popular recreation center until Stanford University bought the land. A walk around the perimeter exposes the birder to five habitats. The lake in winter hosts a variety of ducks, including Ring-necked and Wood Ducks. The tule areas near the wooden bridge are good spots for Common Moorhens. Osprey and Merlin are occasionally seen. The Belted Kingfisher is a resident and frequently perches by the shore. In riparian areas by the lake look for Red-shouldered Hawks.

Chaparral is dominant on west- and south-facing slopes. Resident birds include Wrentits, Bewick's Wrens, and California Thrashers. Blue-gray Gnatcatchers can be detected in spring and summer by their high wheezy scolds.

Forest dominates the canyons and north-facing slopes, including a small grove of redwoods. In winter look for Varied Thrushes and Winter Wren. Year-round residents include Chestnut-backed Chickadee, Bushtit, and Brown Creeper.

The blue oak woodland sits at the top of the ridge. This area is one of the best in the reserve. A special treat is the six species of woodpeckers possible: Hairy, Downy, Acorn, Nuttall's, Northern Flicker, and Red-breasted Sapsucker. White-breasted Nuthatches, various tits, and Dark-eyed Juncos feed in the foliage. In winter, the woodland is an impressive feeding area for migrant Cedar Waxwings and American Robins. On the edge of the grassland, look for Western Bluebirds flycatching in the bare oak branches.

The famous serpentine grasslands are accessible from the lake area by climbing uphill on the fire road, or by a gate in the residential section of Portola Valley. These areas are famed for their rare plants, spring wildflower displays, and rare butterflies. Winter raptors abound. Scan the hilltops for Black-shouldered Kite and the huge, dark form of the Golden Eagle. Other grassland birds include Say's Phoebe, Savannah Sparrows, and Western Bluebirds. Watch for the Bobcats that lie in the grass or prowl for gophers on the fire road.

Directions: Jasper Ridge must be seen with a guide at hand. The Sequoia and Santa Clara Valley Audubon Societies give field trips occasionally. If these do not fit your schedule, call the Jasper Ridge Office at 415-497-1589 and a tour with a docent can be arranged. Donations for the maintenance of this biological wonderland are vastly appreciated!

The preserve lies between the towns of Woodside and Portola Valley, on the west side of Highway 280. The main gate is off Sand Hill Road. The guide will give more specific directions to a gate, depending on what habitat you wish to see.

Special notes: The main function of the preserve is scientific research, not only in biology but in water chemistry, geology, and even archeology. Don't miss the opportunity to ask questions about the research plots you pass. There are restrooms and picnic tables by the lake if you want to eat lunch. No garbage is to be left on the land; take out what you bring in.

The varied landforms, flowers, and scenic vistas make a camera a must on your trip. If you want to see other forms of life, docents have excursions to see flowers, trees, reptiles and amphibians, fungi, etc. The purpose of Jasper Ridge is to provide information, so don't hesitate to ask.

— Sharon Hom

SOUTH COAST

San Mateo County birders boast freely about the bird-richness of the area along the Pacific Coast from Half Moon Bay to Point Ano Nuevo. The varied habitats, encompassing ocean, fresh-water marsh, chaparral, dunes, rocky coast, redwoods, and mixed forests, contain a fascinating array of species year-round. This area has been watched carefully for many years, notably by Sequoia Audubon checklist compiler Peter Metropulos and Christmas Count Compiler Barry Sauppe. Their vigilance has paid off with a number of county records of rare species.

The areas listed under South Coast are all within a short distance of each other, and many form loop journeys that provide a full day's birding.

Pescadero Marsh

If local birders had to choose a single favorite locality for observing birds on the San Francisco Peninsula, it is very likely that the prize would go to Pescadero Marsh. Situated directly on the Pacific Flyway, it serves as an important stop-over point for migrant shorebirds, a wintering ground for numerous waterfowl, and a breeding area for a variety of marsh birds. Pescadero Marsh is a rare and valuable habitat, being the only sizable marsh on the California coast between San Francisco Bay and Monterey County. A rich and diverse combination of habitats occurs here and visitors will enjoy excellent birding at all seasons. Birding is, however, most exciting in fall and winter when birds are most abundant and the likelihood of finding a rarity is greatest.

American Bittern — Cliff Richer

The marsh suffered from heavy siltation during the major winter storms of 1982 and 1983. During 1983 and 1984, members of the Sequoia Audubon Society have been working to reverse the storms' detrimental effects on the marsh in a variety of ways, from organizing trail-clearing parties to working closely with the State Parks and Recreation Department in exploring ways to solve the siltation problems. The marsh must be kept in its former state in order to attract the diversity of bird life it has been known for.

Resident birds, breeding in the marsh, include Pied-billed Grebe, Great Blue Heron, American Bittern, Mallard, Cinnamon Teal, Gadwall, Ruddy Duck, American Coot, Virginia Rail, Black-

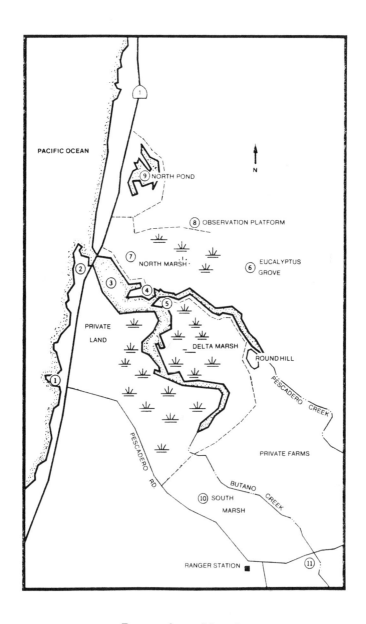

Pescadero Marsh

shouldered Kite, Northern Harrier, Black Phoebe, Marsh Wren, Common Yellowthroat, and Savannah and Song Sparrows. In winter, a few hundred ducks congregate in the marsh; the majority are dabblers but there is also a small number of diving ducks, such as goldeneyes, Bufflehead, scaup, Canvasbacks, and Ring-necked Ducks. This is the time to check for the occasional stray goose or swan. Some of the more uncommon raptors such as Golden Eagle, Osprey, Merlin, and Peregrine Falcon are observed here each fall and winter. Regular winter residents include Great and Snowy Egrets, Black-crowned Night-Heron, Sora, Say's Phoebe, Water Pipit, Common Snipe, and Lincoln's Sparrow. Rare elsewhere in our area in winter, swallows may often be found in the marsh, mainly Violet-green and Tree Swallows. A few White-throated Swifts are usually present with the wintering swallows.

Fall migration is the season when unusual migrant shorebirds are apt to be found. From early August through October, a keen observer could tally 30 or more species of shorebirds at Pescadero Marsh and the adjoining beach. Of course, the number of these birds present will depend upon availability of mudflats. Conditions are best when ponds and the estuary are shallow and large portions of mudflat are exposed. In fall, virtually any shorebird in western North America could show up here, and extreme rarities have been recorded (Ruff, Curlew Sandpiper, Stilt Sandpiper, Sharp-tailed Sandpiper). Species considered rare in our area but which are regular and to be expected in small numbers at Pescadero Marsh each fall are Lesser Golden-Plover (September), Lesser Yellowlegs (August-October), Solitary Sandpiper (early September), Semipalmated Sandpiper (August-early September), Baird's Sandpiper (August-early October), Pectoral Sandpiper (August-early November), Wilson's Phalarope (July-September), and Red Phalarope (late October-early December).

Where to Bird

1. and 2. Parking Lots

Most birding trips start at one or the other of these parking lots. After you cross Pescadero Creek Bridge on Route 1 and climb up the hill you will come to the entrance of the north parking lot on the right. At the time of this writing there is no fee for this lot. If you continue on Route 1, you will soon see a sign for Pescadero Road. The south parking lot is opposite Pescadero Road. A fee is charged for the use of this unpaved lot. However, if you arrive before the attendant or if the lot is uncrowded and you have an understanding attendant, you may park for a short time while you are birding without paying the fee. Do not press the point, however, as this is a courtesy and the attendant has the right to ask for the parking fee.

1. South Parking Lot

Set up your scope at the southwest corner of the parking lot and scan the rock formations. Except during the summer, American Black Oystercatcher are nearly certain here. During the nesting season, they are present in the area but tend to be more secretive. This is also a regular spot for Rock Sandpiper and Wandering Tattler. The Rock Sandpiper often associates with the similar but much larger Surfbirds or with the much darker Black Turnstones. The field guides indicate that the Rock Sandpiper has greenish legs. This is a variable characteristic and the birds we have seen here have yellow legs. The Wandering Tattler is normally a solitary bird, resembling a small streamlined Willet, and may be seen along the shore, on the rocks, or flying up from the rocks whenever a wave breaks over them. Scoters, loons, cormorants, and murres may be seen in the water, and Marbled Murrelet is possible.

2. North Parking Lot

If you cannot get a fee waiver at the south parking lot, it is no great problem. Park at the north lot and walk back. The north lot itself has some birding potential. From the northeast corner, you can get an overview of the marsh and orient yourself with respect to the accompanying map. With a scope you may even be able to identify the terns on the sandbar in the lagoon (Forster's year-round, Caspian spring through fall, Elegant in the fall, perhaps even Least, Common, or Arctic in migration or post-breeding dispersal). Examine the beach below for shorebirds and then walk along one of the many paths to the bluffs overlooking the ocean. The same birds may be seen from here as from the south parking lot, although they are less likely and will probably be further away.

3. The Lagoon

Now much shallower than in the past, the lagoon still has a relatively deep channel which attracts both fresh and saltwater diving birds. Belted Kingfishers and Northern Rough-winged

Swallows have nested in the bluffs above the lagoon for the past several years. The sandbar referred to above is located at the head of the lagoon and offers a roosting place not only for the terns but for gulls and shorebirds as well. At low tide, the shorebirds are more apt to be on the lagoon's mudflats. Baird's, Pectoral, and Semipalmated Sandpipers and Lesser Golden-Plover have all been reported here. Elegant Terns are almost always present here from late July through October — they are noisy and easy to see. A pair or two of Snowy Plovers are often in the area and succeed in breeding here in some years.

4. The Spring

Soon after you turn left into the marsh, you will see a small pool on your left. This freshwater pool is apparently spring-fed and is a good spot for Common Yellowthroats and American Bitterns.

5. The Confluence

To your right, Butano and Pescadero Creeks join together before flowing into the lagoon. Generally, whenever two bodies of water come together, conditions favor those creatures that feed on the smaller aquatic life. Waders, dabblers, divers, and shorebirds may all be found here at times. At high tide when the mudflats are covered, this area can be quite productive. Proceed a short way up Pescadero Creek on the dike checking the shoreline carefully.

6. The Rookery

From anywhere on the dike you can look across the North Marsh to the eucalyptus grove. Great Blue Herons have nested here for the past several years. The nests are relatively low at the approximate midpoint of the grove.

7. The North Marsh

Return toward the highway along the top of the dike, stopping at likely vantage points to scope the marsh. If the water is shallow and mudflats are exposed, this spot is superb in fall for shore-birds. Although the smaller shorebirds will not be identifiable at this distance, you may be rewarded — especially in late fall — with views of Common Moorhen, Common Snipe, and even Virginia Rails feeding in the open. Black-crowned Night-Herons, egrets, and dabbling ducks are usually identifiable as well. Diving ducks are present here in winter when the water is deeper.

Marbled Murrelet — Cliff Richer

8. The Observation Point

Walk north along the highway until you come to a trail which crosses a small causeway between the marsh and North Pond. Although the climb looks imposing it is quite easy and is facilitated by steps set into the hillside. Birding from the observation platform itself is usually poor because of the distances involved and the angle of the sun, but the view is worth the climb and it is a pleasant spot for a moment's respite from a hard day of birding. It is most worthwhile to check here in late afternoon when light conditions are optimum. Look down on North Marsh (preferably with a spotting scope) to examine waterfowl, herons, and shorebirds. Scan the skies above and below for hawks and swallows. Purple Martins are regularly seen here from May until early September, and swifts are a good possibility as well.

9. The North Pond

Either on your way up to the observation platform or on the way back (or both), check the North Pond. Small divers, dabbling ducks, and coots can be seen on the surface. Shorebirds feed along the edges and small islands afford resting places for gulls (including Bonaparte's), terns, shorebirds, and ducks. Great numbers of phalaropes have been seen here in fall. Don't neglect the marsh on the other side of the causeway.

10. South Marsh

Return to your car and drive south to Pescadero Road. Take a left on Pescadero Road. In about a mile the road will run along the edge of the marsh. There are a number of turnoffs in this area where you can pull over and look over the marsh and Butano

Creek. The damage from siltation is more obvious here than in most other areas and the cattail growth is now much heavier than in the past. Nevertheless, wherever the view is unobstructed you should see an astonishing variety of ducks and shorebirds. This is a good spot for American Bitterns, rails, and an occasional Common Moorhen. Look through groups of teal for Blue-winged Teal which are regular here in migration. Scan the higher grassy and weedy areas for Black-shouldered Kites, Northern Harriers, Black Phoebes, and Loggerhead Shrikes. Common Barn-Owls can be heard here during most evenings.

11. Butano Creek Bridge

Continue driving east on Pescadero Road until you come to the ranger station. Take a right onto Bean Hollow Road and park. Walk to the bridge over Butano Creek on Pescadero Road. The riparian growth along the creek has been under-birded due to questions of property lines and the lack of a clearly defined trail, but this area could prove rewarding, especially during migration. Birders in this area have been both welcomed and threatened at different times by property owners.

Directions: From anywhere on the peninsula, take the Bayshore Freeway (Highway 101) or Interstate 280 to Highway 92. Take 92 west to Half Moon Bay and follow it to the end. Turn south (left) on the Coastal Highway (Route 1) and in approximately 15 miles you will see signs for Pescadero State Beach. The marsh is on the opposite side of the road from the beach. Parking is allowed on the road but rules seem to vary from year to year, so obey the signs.

Facilities: There are portable toilets at both the south parking lot and the first parking lot for Pescadero Beach (across from North Pond). The nearby town of Pescadero has a gas station and restaurants, including Duarte's Tavern, frequented by locals for its artichoke soup and olallieberry pie.

Fee: There is a parking fee at the south parking lot.

Nearby points of interest: See other South Coast descriptions.

Special notes: If you are in a hurry or if you are just passing by, you should concentrate your attention on three areas that can be seen from the highway. At low tide you should be able to see and identify (with the help of a good spotting scope) most of the expected marsh species at the lagoon (#3), on North Pond (#9), or in South Marsh (#10). Dress in layers for changeable coastal weather.

Publications: Sequoia Audubon Society has a checklist of the birds of Pescadero Marsh; contact the chapter office for details.

— Cliff Richer
Peter Metropulos

South Coast Back Roads: Searching for Grasshopper Sparrows

The Grasshopper Sparrow is notorious for its irregularity of occurrence, being found in fair numbers at a given locality one year, then perhaps totally absent the next. Hay-cutting practices obviously alter the distribution and nesting success of this species since grass-cutting virtually eliminates this bird's specialized habitat.

A few locations where Grasshopper Sparrows have been noted in several years are outlined below.

Stage Road: From Coastal Route 1 drive two miles inland on Pescadero Road to the small town of Pescadero. Turn left on Stage Road and head north through the "downtown" and continue past the cemetery. Grassy hillsides on the east side of the road from this point on should be checked for Grasshopper Sparrows from April through July. The most reliable spot has been the portion of the road which begins to climb a gradual hill two or three miles from the Pescadero Road junction. This is just north of a large farmhouse (2400 Stage Road). Continue to the top of the hill a mile or so from here, stopping whenever possible to check suitable habitat along the road. The bird is small, dull-colored, and inconspicuous, so its detectability relies upon its song. Listen carefully for the Grasshopper Sparrow's buzzy, insectlike song. They are easiest to locate on mornings when there is no wind. The singing bird is often perched on top of a low bush among the grassland, or occasionally on a barbed wire fence along the road.

It should be noted that Stage Road offers good birding and pleasant countryside but since all land here is private, birding is limited to the roadside.

Another area to check for Grasshopper Sparrows is along **Cloverdale Road.** This is reached by taking Pescadero Road east for two and a half miles from Route 1. Take Cloverdale Road south and check the grassy hillsides along the east side of the road.

If you try all the above locations and still cannot find the birds, go north to **San Gregorio Road** (Highway 84) and head east, stopping along the roadside wherever suitable habitat occurs. The gently sloping grassy hillsides from one to five miles inland on the north side of the road are usually the most productive.

— Peter Metropulos

Cloverdale Road Loop

Cloverdale Road Loop provides a good variety of birding very close to Pescadero Marsh on Coastal Route 1. Upon leaving Pescadero Marsh continue east (inland) on Pescadero Road through the small town of Pescadero.

After crossing a bridge the road curves to the right. Just beyond the curve you will find the Phipps Ranch farm stand. Stop at the stand and ask permission to bird the area of the vegetable gardens. In addition to the farm stand, the Phipps family also operates a petting zoo and a "pick-your-own" berry patch, and invests considerable time and creativity in maintaining this particular area. Flowers are planted with the deliberate intention of attracting hummingbirds. There is a small aviary with Ringed Turtle-Doves and a larger aviary is being constructed for other exotics.

The farm stand is one of the best in the area and is well worth a visit on its own merits. It is normally open at 10 *a.m.,* seven days a week except from December through February. If you arrive before the stand is open feel free to leave you car in the lot but park away from the stand so as to leave room for the regular customers.

The area to be birded is actually a small point of land between Pescadero and Honsinger Creeks. To enter the area walk about 50 feet further up the road and enter a gate on the right. Just

American Kestrel — Cliff Richer

beyond the gate are some brushy areas around an old barn on the left and Honsinger Creek on the right. Check here for sparrows and wrens. The vegetable gardens and blackberry bushes further on will yield goldfinches (Lesser and American year-round and possibly Lawrence's in spring migration) and ground-feeding birds.

You will soon come to the herb and flower garden. This is a good place to take advantage of the benches and tables provided and have lunch or just relax for a few minutes while watching the hummers and Northern Orioles. Acorn, Downy, and Nuttall's Woodpeckers can also be found in this area. Without disturbing the vegetable plantings, return along Pescadero Creek on the opposite side and check the riparian growth and underbrush.

Before leaving the farm be sure to check the trees near the stand and the chaparral across the road. A leisurely hour's walk in this area should produce 40 to 60 species depending on the weather and the season.

From the farm stand continue about 150 yards along the road and take your first right. Proceed to the end of this short connector road and take a left. You are now on Cloverdale Road.

Cloverdale Road generally follows along Butano Creek and Little Butano Creek, leading you through a narrow valley of grasslands surrounded by chaparral and oak forest. The valley is good for typical grassland birds and is a wintering ground for large flocks of American Robins. Many raptors winter here although 95% of those seen will be Red-tailed Hawks or American Kestrels. Red-shouldered, Rough-legged, and Ferruginous Hawks are occasional winter visitors, as are Cattle Egrets and Golden Eagles. Tricolored Blackbirds are abundant and seem to be more clannish than elsewhere, not mingling with the large flocks of starlings, and Brewer's and Red-winged Blackbirds as they do elsewhere. The road is approximately seven miles long and for most of its length has wide paved shoulders allowing for easy pull-overs.

After about four miles you will come to Canyon Road on the left. This is a dirt road following Butano Creek into the climax redwood forest. This road should be explored if you have time. Birding is typically slow in climax forest but the few species which might be seen are Pileated Woodpeckers and American Dippers (both rare in the area, but known to be there), Red-breasted Sapsuckers, Golden-crowned Kinglets, Western Flycatchers, (summer), Hammond's Flycatchers (uncommon, summer) and the more abundant juncos and Steller's Jays. Be sure to check the small clearings along either side of the road as these transitional areas usually have the highest level of avian activity.

Return to Cloverdale Road and continue east past the entrance to Butano State Park. The road now becomes a narrow dirt road — always passable but not always comfortably. For a short while the grassland valley continues but then abruptly descends into a mixed conifer and oak woodland.

When you come to an intersection with another dirt road, bear to the right. You are now on Gazos Creek Road.

Directions: Take Coastal Route 1 south to Pescadero Road. This is 15 miles south of the intersection of Highway 92 and Coastal Route 1, or 3 miles south of Highway 84 and Coastal Route 1. Go east on Pescadero Road 2.5 miles to Cloverdale Road.

Facilities: There are chemical toilets at Pescadero Beach and Gazos Creek Beach Coastal Access. Restaurants and service stations can be found at Gazos Creek and in the town of Pescadero.

Nearby points of interest: See descriptions of Pescadero Marsh, Gazos Creek Road, and other South Coast entries.

— Cliff Richer

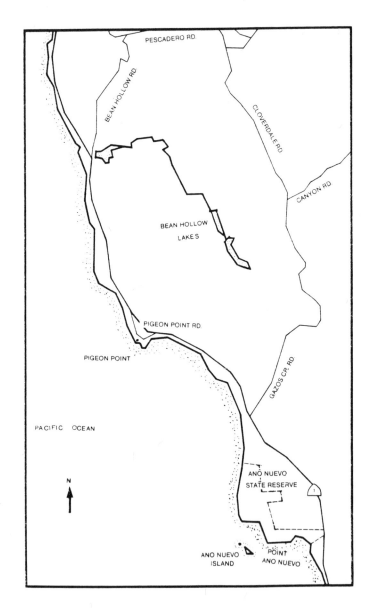

South Coast

Pigeon Point

Pigeon Point, located 50 miles south of San Francisco, is one of the best vantage points for observing seabirds on the Northern California coast. Birding here is extremely variable, ranging from fair to excellent, depending on visibility, season, observer's skill, duration of visit, and wind velocity and direction. Park along the dirt shoulder of Pigeon Point Road anywhere north of the tall, white lighthouse. A good spotting scope is essential because on many days birds are far offshore. By slowly and repeatedly scanning the sea from surf to horizon, a patient birder is often rewarded. The best time of day for bird study is morning, when light conditions are most favorable. The prime time of the year is during spring migration (March-May) when multitudes of north-bound loons, Brant, scoters, phalaropes, terns, gulls, and alcids pass this promontory. A daily census of migrant seabirds passing the point in spring 1976 by Barry Sauppe recorded over *one million* birds! However, to observe large numbers of unusual species here, the wind must be fairly strong (15+ miles per hour) and come from the west or northwest. When the weather is calm or the wind is from the east or northeast, birding can be unexciting.

During low tide, a few American Black Oystercatchers (resident) may be found on the rocks, as well as Wandering Tattlers (August-May), Surfbirds (September-April), and Black Turnstones (year-round). The rare Rock Sandpiper is a possibility here. Pigeon Point is one of the most reliable spots, at least in spring and summer, for finding Marbled Murrelets. The species is more or less resident in the area, and a few pairs may be found feeding just beyond the surf on most days when the surf is not too rough. They can be more difficult to see following the post-breeding dispersal. From November to February, Ancient Murrelets are often seen here, just offshore. During the summer months feeding masses of Sooty Shearwaters seen from the point may number in the tens of thousands.

The following list enumerates some of the more uncommon and local seabirds, including their status, seasonal occurrence, and additional information, observed from Pigeon Point, 1974-1984:

Yellow-billed Loon: One, migrant in breeding plumage, May 9, 1979.

Black-footed Albatross: Uncommon but regular, March-May. Usually seen following large ships. Up to 20 have been seen in a day here.

Laysan Albatross: Two records, March 30, 1979, and March 29, 1984. Both following ships.

Northern Fulmar: Highly irregular in numbers, though regular in appearance in winter and early spring.

Pink-footed Shearwater: Fairly common, late April-October.

Buller's Shearwater: Uncommon but regular August-October.

Black-vented Shearwater: Erratic in occurrence, most regular in fall and spring when 100+ have been seen in a day. Several winter records.

Sooty Shearwater: Common, February-November. Often seen close to shore.

Short-tailed Shearwater: Rare but probably regular here in winter and early spring; recorded here between November 12 and March 16. High count of eight birds.

Ashy Storm-Petrel: One, May 5, 1976, is the only record.

Red Phalarope: Uncommon to common, spring and fall, peak in late May. Erratic in occurrence. High count of over 20,000 birds on May 20, 1980.

Parasitic Jaeger: Uncommon but regular, August-November, less common April-May. Usually seen in pursuit of gulls or terns.

Pomarine Jaeger: Uncommon, April-May, one or two being seen here on most days. Also uncommon July-October. This is the jaeger most often seen here.

Long-tailed Jaeger: One, October 13, 1976, is the only record.

Black-legged Kittiwake: Erratic in numbers, but may be fairly common at times, March-May. High count of 264 on May 15, 1976. Stragglers recorded here at all times of year.

Sabine's Gull: Uncommon to rare in May. Surprisingly high count of 323 in late May 1976.

Little Gull: One, April 19, 1979, is the only record.

Glaucous Gull: Three spring records between March 18 and May 22.

Arctic Tern: Uncommon in late spring (May). Dozens have been seen in a day.

Common Tern: Uncommon to fairly common late April to mid-May.

Elegant Tern: Fairly common, July-October. Small groups seen daily in season.

Pigeon Guillemot: Fairly common, March-September. Rare in midwinter. A few pairs nest on cliffs near lighthouse.

Tufted Puffin: Rare but regular May-July, close to shore. Suspected of nesting on Ano Nuevo Island.

Rhinocerous Auklet: Uncommon. Has been seen at all times of year but most common in midwinter. A feeding flock of 300 birds was here February 13, 1976.

Cassin's Auklet: Rarely seen here, though there are records for every season.

Besides seabirds, Pigeon Point can also be a good spot for migrant land birds. Check the weedy edges of the brussels sprouts field along the road for finches. Rarities such as Ground Dove, Tropical Kingbird, Bobolink, Palm Warbler, Lark Bunting, Yellow-headed Blackbird, and Clay-colored Sparrow have been seen here. There are often a few Band-tailed Pigeons on the wires, especially in the morning. (Pigeon Point, however, was not named for its pigeons but rather in memory of the U.S.S. Pigeon, a ship that crashed into the rocks here early this century.) Huge flocks of Tricolored Blackbirds may be found all year in the plowed fields and cow pastures of this area.

Directions: Take Coastal Route 1 to Pigeon Point Road, a little over six miles south of well-marked Pescadero Beach. The nearest large towns are Half Moon Bay, 20 miles to the north, and Santa Cruz, 25 miles to the south.

Facilities: Overnight accommodations are available at Pigeon Point Youth Hostel; call 415-879-0633 for reservations and information. A restaurant and gas station (hours and days open vary) are located at Gazos Creek, two miles to the south. Portable toilets are located at Gazos Creek Beach Coastal Access and at Pescadero Beach.

Nearby points of interest: See other South Coast descriptions.

Special notes: A spotting scope is essential here. Dress warmly.

— Peter Metropulos

Gazos Creek Road

Gazos Creek Road begins on the east side of Coastal Route 1 nine miles south of Pescadero Beach, directly opposite the sign designating "Gazos Creek Beach Coastal Access." You have the option of either parking your vehicle at the beach parking lot and traversing the road on foot, or driving slowly up the road and stopping at any of the several dirt turnouts along the way. The first two miles of the road are most productive for birding. Here you will find yourself entering a cool, moist coastal canyon with hillsides of thick chaparral and scrub, and scattered groves of Douglas fir and live oaks. The shallow, rocky creek is bordered by a dense riparian woodland of alder, willow, and elderberry. A wide variety of ferns, berries, and flowering shrubs occupy the woodland understory and spanish moss hangs from oak limbs above, creating a peaceful and luxuriant setting for a day afield.

During sunny summer weekends, a moderate amount of traffic and resultant dust clouds on the dirt road may put a damper on pleasurable walking, but birding in early mornings, weekdays, or off-season months is almost always rewarding, not only for birds, but also for plants and other forms of wildlife. Birding is best during the breeding season (March-August) when birds are on territory in full song. Expect to find a thorough representation of typical coastal woodland species. Walking along the road is the best bird-finding strategy since birds are most conspicuous along the forest edge. A list of some of the expected bird species is given below:

Common Year-round Residents: Band-tailed Pigeon, Belted Kingfisher, Hairy and Downy Woodpeckers, Northern Flicker, Black Phoebe, Winter and Bewick's Wren, Brown Creeper, Hutton's Vireo, Purple Finch, Pine Siskin

Common Breeding Birds (March-August): White-throated Swift, Allen's Hummingbird, Olive-sided Flycatcher, Western Wood-Pewee, Western Flycatcher, Violet-green Swallow, Swainson's Thrush, Warbling Vireo, Orange-crowned and Wilson's Warblers, Black-headed Grosbeak

Winter Residents: Red-breasted Sapsucker, Varied and Hermit Thrushes, Cedar Waxwing, Townsend's Warbler, Fox and Lincoln's Sparrows

Western Screech Owls — Cliff Richer

Uncommon Summer Visitors (most of these wander downslope from breeding sites at higher elevations nearby and occur regularly in small numbers each summer): Vaux's Swift, Purple Martin, Red-breasted Nuthatch, Golden-crowned Kinglet, MacGillivray's, Hermit, Yellow-rumped, and Black-throated Gray Warblers, Red Crossbill

Two miles inland, Gazos Creek Road will form a junction with Cloverdale Road (also dirt). Cloverdale Road winds north through open grassland toward Butano State Park and the town of Pescadero. From the junction east, Gazos Creek Road begins to ascend gradually into the Santa Cruz Mountains. The canyon becomes steeper and narrower and the woods deeper and darker, the creek more turbulent, and the bird life not as varied as below. It would be worthwhile for adventurous individuals to drive up the road and see how far you can get. The road becomes rough and full of potholes, and is often closed here in wet winter months. Driving should be undertaken with caution since the road becomes narrow and logging trucks may appear anywhere around the next bend. Hiking here, however, is quite pleasant. Dense coniferous forest dominates the canyon most of the way. Check the rocky sections of the creek for American Dippers which regularly nest here. Although not to be expected, some of the rarer forest species such as Pileated Woodpecker and Spotted Owl have been observed along this stretch of road. The road continues uphill for several miles and eventually enters Big Basin State Park at over 2000' elevation. At the summit is a dry, rocky stand of Knobcone Pine and Manzanitas, a unique plant community in this area. Bird life here is not as abundant but there is the possibility of something unusual here since the habitat is atypical of the region. Breeding species here include Common Poorwill, Western Screech-Owl, Black-throated Gray Warbler, Solitary Vireo, and Red Crossbill.

Nighttime owling anywhere along Gazos Creek Road can be excellent. Great Horned, Pygmy, and Common Barn-Owls are commonly heard and seen here. Western Screech-Owls (open oaks) and Northern Saw-whet Owls (deep forest) are uncommon and harder to find although probably resident. A few Spotted and Long-eared Owls have been found here in recent years, but should be considered quite rare. Common Poorwills are fairly common summer residents on the higher chaparral-covered slopes above the canyon and may be heard calling on calm, warm summer nights.

A number of rare, out-of-range migrant songbirds from the East Coast have been sighted along Gazos Creek during late spring (late May-June) and birders should be aware of the possibility of finding such rare "treasures." Hooded Warbler, Black-and-white Warbler, Northern Parula, Yellow-breasted Chat, Rose-breasted Grosbeak, and Indigo Bunting have been recorded here in recent years.

Directions: Take Coastal Route 1 nine miles south of Pescadero Beach, which is south of Half Moon Bay and San Francisco and north of Santa Cruz.

Facilities: There is a gas station and a restaurant on Route 1 across from Gazos Beach. (Note: during winter months, the gas station is closed more often than not.)

Nearby points of interest: See other entries for South Coast areas.

— Peter Metropulos

Ano Nuevo State Reserve

Ano Nuevo State Reserve is one of the most picturesque and ecologically rich areas along the central California coast. Primarily a marine life reserve, the park boasts sweeping dunes, sheer cliffs, panoramic views of the Santa Cruz Mountains, an intricate plant community, fascinating intertidal marine life, breeding elephant seals, and a varied and unique bird community.

The land that now encompasses the reserve had a long and colorful human history, beginning with the sighting of Point Ano Nuevo by the Vizcaino expedition in 1603 and subsequently passing through several different owners' hands, including millworkers and dairy and cattle ranchers. The area began to resemble its present state in 1958 when the state of California bought a large portion of the land; it continued to buy adjoining parcels through 1979. Ano Nuevo State Reserve is best known to the public at large as the breeding grounds for thousands of Northern Elephant Seals every winter from November through March. Since 1975, student guides from the University of Santa

Willet — Cliff Richer

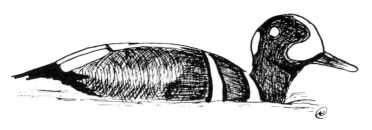

Harlequin Duck — Cliff Richer

Cruz have led visitors on tours of the breeding grounds through a special reservations-only program. This program protects the public and the seals from each other and serves to educate visitors about the reserve and its inhabitants as well.

Access to most of the reserve during winter is limited to these guided walks, though birders can walk the trails to just beyond the freshwater pond without tour reservations. The remainder of the year, most trails and the point itself are open; permits are required for some areas.

A birding trip here any season of the year is apt to bring rewards. A spotting scope is highly desirable to get close-up views of seabirds and mammals. Be prepared for cool, windy, foggy conditions, even in midsummer. To cover the reserve to its fullest, take a three-mile round trip, beginning at the parking lot and heading west to Point Ano Nuevo. The trail overlooks the ocean, leading first through weedy fields, then through rolling dunes down to the rocky beach. Hiking here is moderately strenuous.

Just east of the parking lot is a wooded area where you can often see typical western forest and scrubland birds. Walk along the road here and keep an eye and ear alert for resident Wrentits, Winter Wrens, Bewick's Wrens, Steller's Jays, Hairy Woodpeckers, Black Phoebes, Hutton's Vireos, and Pygmy Nuthatches. These birds are easiest to find in early morning. Scan the skies here for swallows (all western species) and swifts (Vaux's, White-throated, Black) from spring through fall, and year-round for raptors and Band-tailed Pigeons. Heading west from the parking lot through the fields, there will be a freshwater pond on the right side of the trail which should be checked for ducks, rails, and other water birds. Many very rare vagrant songbirds have been recorded during the fall migration in the willows and weedy edges of the pond. Once west of the pond, one may scan the ocean waters below for grebes, loons, and scoters. Marbled Murrelets are resident here and easiest to see from March through

September, when they are often seen in pairs not far from shore. (Although considered a pelagic species, these small alcids nest, amazing as it may seem, atop tall redwood trees in the nearby Santa Cruz Mountains.) The rocks below the cliffs should be checked for shorebirds such as American Black Oystercatcher, Wandering Tattler, Surfbird, turnstones, and Whimbrel, all of which are present all year except midsummer.

Check this area carefully for Harlequin Ducks, often seen resting on these rocks during low tide. This is the most southerly location where this species is observed regularly, albeit only in small numbers and most reliably in winter. Pelagic Cormorants and Pigeon Guillemots nest on the steep cliffs below the trail and are easy to study in spring and early summer. Bank Swallows and Cliff Swallows maintain breeding colonies on the cliffs, and a few pairs of the rare and local Black Swift nest in sea caves here May through September. The trail continues through a weedy field which should be scanned for Black-shouldered Kite, Northern Harrier, and other resident raptors, as well as Say's Phoebe and Lincoln's Sparrow (both in winter) and other field dwellers.

Once the trail enters the dunes area, take some time to look at the ever-changing plant community. Many colorful coastal wildflowers will be blooming in spring and summer, much to the delight of botanists and hummingbirds alike (Allen's are common here May through August and Anna's are resident). Brush Rabbits will hop out of your way at every bend and California Thrashers often dart roadrunner-style from thicket to thicket.

Once through the dunes, the trail ends at a point on the rocky beach directly across from Ano Nuevo Island. The island is a breeding reserve and study area harboring thousands of seals and sea lions and is strictly off-limits to the public. This is an excellent vantage point from which to spend some time observing birds of the open ocean and rocky coastline. Just to the north is a protected cove which usually has piles of tide-cast seaweed along the shore. Hordes of flies congregate here, attracting a wide variety of gulls and shorebirds, especially during periods of migration. Rarities such as Ruffs, Curlew Sandpipers, Sharptailed Sandpipers, and Buff-breasted Sandpipers have been recorded here, along with small numbers of Baird's and Pectoral Sandpipers and Lesser Golden-Plovers which occur here annually from August to October. In summer and fall, Elegant Terns and Heermann's Gulls can't be missed at Point Ano Nuevo. The protected cove should be checked for Black Scoter, Harlequin Duck, Red-necked Grebe, and Black Brant, all regular here in small numbers. With the use of a spotting scope, Ano Nuevo Island can be scrutinized. Besides the masses of marine mammals lounging on or about the island, gulls, cormorants, and Brown Pelicans roost here by the thousands in summer and fall. Nesting birds on the island include Western Gulls and American Black Oystercatchers. Be on the lookout for alcids in the waters around the island. During the summer, Rhinoceros and Cassin's Auklets and Tufted Puffins are occasionally seen feeding in the vicinity; in the winter, look for Ancient Murrelets.

During spring migration, Gray Whales can regularly be seen heading north often quite close to shore, and, although uncommon this far north, California Sea Otters have been seen here as well.

Directions: Take Coastal Route 1 to New Year's Creek Road where you'll see a sign pointing the short way to the reserve parking lot. This is 17.5 miles south of the junction of Route 1 and Highway 84 at San Gregorio Beach, approximately 58 miles south of San Francisco and 17 miles north of Santa Cruz.

Fee: $2.00 for year-round park use as of 1984 (subject to change); for tickets to elephant seal tours, call TICKETRON in the San Francisco or Santa Cruz areas.

Facilities: The Interpretive Center is open on weekends year-round and on weekdays during elephant seal season; chemical toilets are available, and a catering truck is located on the premises during elephant seal season. Restaurants and gas stations (limited hours open) are located in the nearby towns of Gazos Creek and Pescadero, both north of Ano Nuevo on Route 1. A large range of services is available in Half Moon Bay, 30 minutes north of the reserve at the junction of Route 1 and Highway 92.

Nearby points of interest: See other South Coast entries.

Publications: Those wanting to know more about Ano Nuevo State Reserve may want to read *The Natural History of Ano Nuevo*, Le Boeuf and Kaza, editors. Other publications are available at the Interpretive Center.

— Peter Metropulos
Anne Scanlan-Rohrer

GREATER BAY AREA BIRDING SPOTS

There are several areas outside of the San Francisco Peninsula boundaries that are favorites with local birders. Visitors to the peninsula who have the time to visit any of these spots should make the effort to do so; all of these areas are visited annually or more often by local Audubon chapters.

The **Baylands Nature Preserve** in Palo Alto, at the eastern end of Embarcadero Road off Highway 101, attracts a great number of waterfowl and shorebirds every winter. PG&E catwalks traversing the cordgrass and pickleweed marshland provide good looks at rails, including the endangered California Clapper Rail, Virginia Rail, Sora, and occasional glimpses of the furtive Black Rail. Other species found here include American Bittern, Black-shouldered Kite, Northern Harrier, Western Meadowlark, Common Yellowthroat, Marsh Wren, and sparrows — Song, Savannah, and rarely a Swamp or Sharp-tailed Sparrow. The Lucy Evans Interpretive Center sponsors slide shows, nature walks, and interpretive literature; call 415-329-2506 for more information. *Birding at the Bottom of the Bay* by the Santa Clara Valley Audubon Society (415-329-1811) describes this area and other South Bay areas in detail.

The **San Francisco Bay National Wildlife Refuge** is across the bay from the southern end of the San Francisco Peninsula at the east end of the Dumbarton Bridge (Highway 84). The salt ponds and marshes draw large concentrations of shorebirds fall through spring — most noticeable are the Black-necked Stilts and American Avocets. Black-shouldered Kites are usually seen here, and occasional Burrowing Owls glare from obvious perches. Waterfowl, gulls, terns, and swallows are present at various times of the year. The refuge has an interpretive center (call 415-792-3178 for information on hours open and scheduled nature walks) and a variety of self-guided trails.

Near the wildlife refuge is **Coyote Hills Regional Park.** One of the highlights of this park is a boardwalk leading through the park's freshwater marshes. Many species of dabbling ducks can be seen in the marsh ponds in winter, and it is a good place to search for American Bitterns, Soras, and Common Moorhens hiding in the reeds. The park's other habitats include bay shoreline, grassy hills, fields, and some tree cover. One summer the park hosted a pair of Great Horned Owls and young, a Northern Saw-whet Owl, and a Long-eared Owl, all within a short distance of the park headquarters. From the Dumbarton Bridge, take Jarvis Avenue to Newark Boulevard northwest, then turn onto Patterson Ranch Road; the park is at the end of this road. The Coyote Hills Regional Park headquarters number is 415-471-4967.

The area surrounding the west end of the **Dumbarton Bridge** in San Mateo County formerly drew many of the same species that are found at the refuge, but at this time the area is under development and in a state of change.

Lake Merritt is the artificial lake in downtown Oakland, across the bay from San Francisco. It is only a short distance from Highways 17 and 580. This urban lake is crowded with water birds in the winter, including mergansers, dabbling and diving ducks, grebes, gulls, and cormorants. Rare but regularly seen here most winters are Barrow's Goldeneyes, Oldsquaw, and Hooded Mergansers. The park area around the lake holds a variety of land birds as well, and has drawn Tropical Kingbird and Summer Tanager as vagrants.

Bolinas Lagoon on Shoreline Highway (Coastal Route 1) near Stinson Beach in Marin County, one hour north of San Francisco, is a wonderful haven for shorebirds, dabbling and diving ducks, gulls, and other water birds. Winter brings teal, wigeons, scoters, and mergansers to the lagoon; a flock of Brant can be found at several times during the year; and spring is often heralded by the return of an active pair of Ospreys, frequently seen fishing the lagoon. Located on Shoreline Highway across from the lagoon is **Audubon Canyon Ranch,** an old dairy ranch that is the site of a Great Blue Heron and Great Egret heronry from March through late June each year. The herons and egrets nest in the flattened tops of redwoods and feed in Bolinas Lagoon. Audubon Canyon Ranch is jointly sponsored by the Golden Gate, Sequoia, Marin, and Madrone Audubon Societies. Besides the heronry, the ranch has several miles of hiking trails, a bookstore, natural history museum, and picnic grounds. The Audubon Canyon Ranch organization sponsors a docent program and educational seminars for adults and children. The organization is also developing programs for their Bouverie Audubon Preserve in Sonoma County, and has acquired additional habitat in Marin County near Inverness and Tomales Bay. The ranch is open weekends, 10 *a.m.* to 4 *p.m.*, March 1 through July 4; call 415-383-1644 for more information.

If you continue on Route 1 north to the town of Olema and turn off onto Bear Valley Road, you will come to the headquarters of the **Point Reyes National Seashore.** This area merits a detailed description, found at the end of this section.

Also found in this area is the **Point Reyes Bird Observatory** (415-868-1221). Their Palomarin Field Station is found by following Route 1 to the north end of Bolinas Lagoon, making a sharp left turn onto Olema/Bolinas Road, and turning right onto Mesa road; stay on Mesa heading towards the ocean and you will eventually find the field station. Bird banding demonstrations are held here throughout the year. This station is the center for PRBO's land bird research program.

On the outskirts of the town of Livermore in the East Bay, one hour from the San Francisco Peninsula, is **Mines Road,** a country road winding through a canyon, and a favorite of area birders. Spring is the best time here; regular species include Phainopepla, Wild Turkey, Greater Roadrunner, Lawrence's Goldfinch, Northern Oriole, Lazuli Bunting, and Lewis' Woodpecker. The road reaches the San Antonio Valley junction, where birders can continue over Mount Hamilton and back through San Jose, or turn east on Del Puerto Canyon Road to Interstate 5 and back through Livermore. Both paths provide a good array of birds. This is a standard trip each year for the Golden Gate and Sequoia Audubon Societies. It is best to go with a group the first time to discover the best birding spots along the road.

The birding spots in the **Monterey Bay Area** are one to two and a half hours' drive south of the San Francisco Peninsula. One of the northernmost birding spots in this area is **Elkhorn Slough,** a large coastal estuary near the town of Moss Landing. The slough is a prime area to see wintering waterfowl and shorebirds. Several hundred of the slough's acres are managed by The Nature Conservancy. Information about Elkhorn Slough and the Conservancy's other preserves can be obtained from their California Field Office, 415-777-0487.

The **Monterey Bay** itself attracts a great number of pelagic birds due to its submarine canyon and the abundance of life in its waters. Debra Love Shearwater conducts boat trips on the bay on a year-round basis. Each trip is attended by experienced naturalists. Contact Shearwater Journeys at 408-425-8111 for more information. For the landlubber birder, the wharfs and shoreline of Monterey Bay provide good looks at water birds.

Driving along the coast south from Monterey will take you to Pacific Grove and **Asilomar State Beach,** a beautiful stretch of beach with tidepools and rocky shorelines. Cormorants gather in great numbers on large rock outcroppings here, and it is a good place to scope for grebes, loons, and scoters.

Further south along the coast is the idyllic town of Carmel. The two chief joys for birders here are the **Carmel River** and the various species found at the river mouth and upstream; and the **Point Lobos State Reserve,** with its large breeding colony of Brandt's Cormorants and the diverse mixture of birds found in its forests, meadows, and shoreline.

The **Los Banos Area refuges and Panoche Valley** are usually combined into a weekend birding trip in February by the Sequoia, Golden Gate, and Santa Clara Valley Audubon Societies; as with Mines Road in Livermore, it is preferable to go with a group the first time. The **San Luis and Merced Wildlife Refuges** are south of the San Francisco Peninsula off Interstate 5, about a two and a half hours' drive. The refuges attract thousands of geese and ducks, plus White-faced Ibis, Sandhill Cranes, and raptors. A short drive south of Los Banos on Interstate 5 brings you to road J1 and the Little Panoche Detention Dam. This is the start of the route through **Panoche Valley.** Various stops along J1 can produce Mountain Bluebirds, Lark and Vesper Sparrows, Rock Wren, Chukar, Mountain Plover, Golden Eagle, Prairie Falcon, Greater Roadrunner, Lewis' Woodpecker, and Phainopepla. Birders return on Highway 25 through Hollister to Highway 101 through San Jose.

POINT REYES —
The Outer Point

Point Reyes is a geological oddity. Floating on the tectonic plates that lie on the western side of the San Andreas Fault, it drifts each year two inches further to the north. However, in 1906 the same earthquake that devastated San Francisco caused the point to leap nearly 20 feet in one bound!

To what extent this affects the ecology of Point Reyes or contributes to its unique reputation among birders is purely speculative but it is only one of many features that make Point Reyes the fascinating place that it is.

Within its 100 square miles, Point Reyes contains a diversity of habitats that deserve the birder's attention. Duxbury Reef, Palomarin, Pine Gulch Creek, Five Brooks Trailhead, White House Pool, Shields Salt Marsh, Limantour, Tomales Bay State Park, Abbott's Lagoon, and Pierce Point Road are all well-known areas.

But in the spring and fall, whenever Point Reyes is mentioned the birder thinks of the desolate, windswept, and fog-shrouded outer point. Migratory birds that find their biological direction-finders malfunctioning seek refuge on this last outpost before resuming their tragically errant journeys out to sea. In this apparently inhospitable and naturally treeless land, vagrant and accidental passerines tend to be attracted to the windbreaks planted by ranchers in past years, to protected ponds, or to isolated weed patches. It is here that the rare birds and the birders concentrate.

Where to Bird

The birding spots described below are listed in the order in

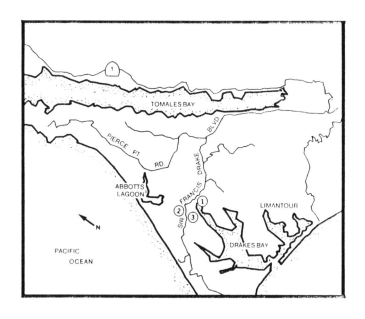

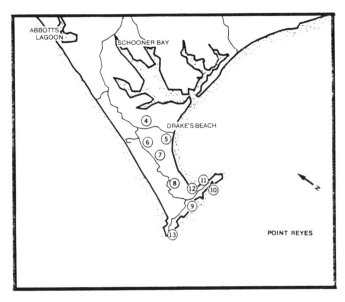

Point Reyes — The Outer Point

which they will be encountered while driving from Inverness out to the lighthouse, but most experienced birders tailor their itinerary according to the weather and the season. A fairly typical itinerary would include a brief stop at Schooner Bay and another at Mendoza Ranch on the way to begin the serious birding day at the lighthouse. After the lighthouse, the fish docks area is the usual next stop, followed by the Nunes Ranch. The best place for lunch is Drake's Beach, which is the most sheltered spot on the point and has picnic tables and even a snack bar. Snack bar hours vary by season and from year to year so it is best to bring some food and liquids for lunch. On most spring and fall weekends you will encounter other birders and it is considered good form to exchange information on sightings. A "good bird" can call for an immediate change in itinerary since it may decide to resume its migration or seek a more isolated location at any time. The sight of a large number of parked cars at a location usually merits investigation since this may indicate a "hot" location or a very unusual sighting.

1. Schooner Bay

Four or five miles beyond the Pierce Point Road intersection, you will see the Johnson Oyster Farm sign. To the left is Schooner Bay where ships once took on lumber and dairy products. Today, the bay is silted in and its mudflats and channels support large numbers of wintering shorebirds and dabbling ducks. The main attraction here, however, is the hillside opposite the bay. Check the utility poles and fence posts carefully as this is one of the most reliable spots for Peregrine Falcons and Merlins (rarer) as well as the more usual American Kestrels and Turkey Vultures. (My experiences here suggest that a Peregrine can probably be expected to make at least a brief appearance at nearly every low tide in the winter.)

2. The Antenna Farms

In another two or three miles you will come to a complex of radio towers on the right. If you are pressed for time, skip this area or bird it on your return. Although Bobolinks and Lesser Golden-Plovers have been seen in the grassy fields surrounding the towers and an occasional eastern warbler has been found in the rows of trees leading to the RCA short wave transmitter, this is a large area requiring a considerable expenditure of time with only a slim chance of any results.

3. The Abandoned Farm

On the opposite side of the road and looking back towards Schooner Bay you will see an isolated grove of trees. This is also a good stop for the return trip. Although yielding an occasional rarity, it is better noted for its resident Bewick's and House Wrens and California Quail. Great Horned Owls nest here and hopefully feed on the multitudinous starlings which have replaced the swallows and Western Bluebirds that formerly nested here. Watch your step — both literally and figuratively — as cattle graze actively in the area.

4. The Hall Ranch

Continue on Sir Francis Drake Boulevard for three or four miles to the Drake's Beach turnoff. Turn left. If the grass is not too high in the fields on either side of the intersection, they may be worth checking in fall or winter for longspurs or Lesser Golden-Plovers. A short way further on the right you will see a natural history marker just off the road. From this vantage point you can look out over the fields below. Check the utility poles as Ferruginous Hawk is a regular winter visitor and is most often seen in this area. A short distance to the northwest (to your right as you look out over the valley) there is a small pond. This area is often overlooked but has yielded Pectoral Sandpiper and Tufted Duck in the past. A few hundred yards further down the road and on the opposite side is the Hall Ranch itself. The muddy and torn-up farmyard has been the usual place to find longspurs who associate with the many Horned Larks normally found here in the winter. For the past several years a lone Eurasian Skylark has also wintered here. You are allowed to enter the fields to get a closer look or to search beyond the ridgetops. (This is true of most of the agricultural fields at Point Reyes. Except at the Nunes Ranch, the rules are: cows and cowhands have the right of way; farm buildings and their immediate surroundings are off-limits; handle fences carefully; close all gates behind you; and clean your boots before you get back into the car. NOTE: Point Reyes dairy cattle are placid beasts and will often follow birders out of curiosity, and not with malice aforethought. Bulls have been rendered nearly obsolete by artificial insemination and, in any case, would not be pastured with the other cattle. However, good sense dictates that you should give a wide berth to any cows with calves.)

Park rules require that you park with all four wheels off the road. This is not usually a problem except in extremely wet years or immediately following a rain. (At those times check the shoulders very carefully before pulling over.)

5. Drake's Beach

Continuing down the road, you will soon come to Drake's Beach which is more prized for clean restrooms and its snack bar than for birds. The parking lot is good for close-up studies of a variety of gulls and Glaucous Gulls are sometimes seen on the beach in winter. Co.. non Ravens nest in the trees at the northeast corner of the parking lot and the pond and marsh at the northwest corner are worth a look. If you have not already seen Tricolored Blackbirds by this time, you should be able to pick a few out from the Red-winged Blackbirds at this site.

6. The Spaletta Ranch

Retrace your route back to Sir Francis Drake Boulevard and turn left. The first farm you come to is the Spaletta Ranch. Birding here is highly variable and few rare birds linger here for more than

Peregrine Falcon — Cliff Richer

a few hours. Starlings, House Sparrows, blackbirds and House Finches dominate the local bird life and probably present more competition than the typical migrant can handle. However, the fields on the left just beyond the farm buildings and all the way to the top of the second ridge (marked by a sign reading "Point Reyes Test Range") have been a traditional wintering ground for a small flock of Lesser Golden-Plovers.

7. The Mendoza Ranch

Continuing approximately 2.5 miles down the road you will come to the Mendoza Ranch. Stop just before you come to the farm buildings and scan the pond to the left and below. The Pectoral Sandpiper is a regular here in the fall and many other rarities have been reported. The trees immediately to the right have a deserved reputation as a "warbler trap" and should be checked carefully. Most of the small birds here will be House Sparrows or House Finches but you may be rewarded with a glimpse of something worthwhile.

8. The Nunes Ranch

In another mile and a half or so you will come to one of the premier birding spots on the Point. Parking here is quite limited and if you are with a large group or if there are other birders in the area, you may have to drive beyond the ranch, park at the Chimney Rock Road intersection and walk back. *Do not park in the ranch yard or block any gates.* By agreement with the rancher you are allowed to bird the area immediately north of the farmhouse but must stay under the trees and out of the fields or farmyard. Bird this area carefully and thoroughly and be sure to scan the marshy fields beyond the trees and behind the farmhouses. An amazing variety of birds has been reported from this one grove of trees. On a "hot" weekend in the fall there may be a half dozen rare species flitting overhead and you may overhear "heavy duty" birders debating leg and toe pad color as a means of distinguishing Bay-breasted and Blackpoll warblers or be treated to a lecture on the significance of tail spots in warbler identification.

9. Road Fork Pool

Just beyond and above the Nunes Ranch is a narrow paved road leading off to the left. This is Chimney Rock Road. Take a left onto it and park immediately. Just above the intersection is a small spring-fed pool and marsh. This area and the rocky terraces above it have produced Clay-colored and Swamp Sparrows, a Scissor-tailed Flycatcher, Sage Thrashers, and other vagrants in recent years.

After leaving this area continue on Chimney Rock Road, scanning the flocks of blackbirds in the fields below you. One or two Rusty Blackbirds are reported from this area almost every fall.

10. The Fish Docks

Park in the lot at the end of the public section of Chimney Rock Road. The road continues beyond this point but vehicle access is limited to park officials and permit holders. Scan the bay for scoters (Black Scoter is resident in the area), loons, Pigeon Guillemots, and diving ducks.

This area is relatively sheltered from the wind and the ranger's residence is surrounded by the largest grove of trees on the outer point. For these reasons, this area has probably produced the largest number of vagrant and accidental sightings on the point. Great Horned Owls, Western Bluebirds, and Pine Siskins are resident and Yellow-rumped Warblers are numerous in fall and winter. Check the trees carefully but stay out of the ranger's front yard and garden.

East of the house behind a small utility shed is a brushy draw which is especially good in the spring. Rose-breasted Grosbeaks can be found here almost every spring and Gray Foxes have established dens in the underbrush in past years. Further east there is an isolated line of pines along the road to Chimney Rock. These should also be checked.

11. Chimney Rock

Trails lead east from both the parking lot and the residence to Chimney Rock. Any of these will eventually take you to the windy observation point (approximately one mile uphill, but a fairly easy climb) where you can scan Chimney Rock and other offshore rocks for American Black Oystercatchers, nesting Western Gulls and perhaps Tufted Puffins. Puffins formerly nested here and were sighted regularly from this spot. There were some indications that there was another nesting attempt in the spring of 1984 after an absence of several years.

12. The New Willows

After returning to the fish docks, you should explore this area approximately half a mile to the west of the parking lot. This area is reached via a narrow footpath originating from the widest part of the road below the parking area. There is no climbing to speak of but footing may be treacherous, particularly in wet weather, and boots are recommended for ankle support. The New Willows is actually a gully which extends from the beach back towards the Nunes Ranch. This draw is filled with young riparian growth and seems to be productive when other areas are a washout. In recent years, Gray Catbirds and Veeries have been spotted here. Just below the New Willows is a small protected cove where scoters haul out to rest on the beach. Oldsquaws have been seen here on occasion.

13. The Lighthouse

Retrace your route back to Sir Francis Drake Boulevard and take a left proceeding on to the end of the road. Park in the designated areas and then walk uphill along the road beyond the gate. Surrounded on three sides by the Pacific Ocean, often obscured by fog and almost always beset by fierce winds, this bleak area has probably produced the largest variety of vagrant and accidental bird species on the West Coast. As you proceed

Tufted Puffin — Cliff Richer

uphill watch the ocean below for Pigeon Guillemots and Common Murres, and the rocks above for Rock Wrens — both year-round residents. Shortly you will come to a line of gnarled cypresses. Bird these trees with painstaking care, both on the way up and on the way back. Check the slopes beyond and above the trees and the weed patches behind the ranger residences.

Go on to the observation platform. Look straight down on the south side (on your left as you approach the platform) and scan the ocean below for Tufted Puffins or other unusual alcids. There was good evidence that puffins were nesting directly below this spot in 1984 and other alcids are sometimes seen in the air or on the water below the observation point. If you look straight down from the north side of the platform you will see the rocks harboring the Common Murre nesting colony. Brown Pelicans, American Black Oystercatchers, three species of cormorants and at least four species of gulls can usually be seen sharing these and neighboring rocks. During the nesting season, Common Ravens often lurk here looking for the opportunity to steal an unguarded egg. Sabine's Gulls are occasionally seen flying by.

One of the most unusual manmade features here is the lighthouse itself which is situated below the point, nearly at sea level. If you have an interest in old lighthouses or want to show off your physical conditioning, you can walk down the hundreds of steps to visit it. Although it is now automated, most of the old equipment has been preserved and the park rangers conduct guided tours. Check at the small visitor center between the residences and the observation platform to be sure that the lighthouse is open to the public before committing yourself as it is often closed because of weather or temporary staff shortages.

Directions: From the San Francisco Peninsula, take Interstate 280 to Daly City and exit left to Route 1 (19th Avenue). Proceed north across the Golden Gate Bridge on State Highway 101 and continue to the San Quentin exit (approximately eight miles). After exiting, turn left. You are now on Sir Francis Drake Boulevard, which continues all the way to the Point Reyes Lighthouse, at land's end of the outer point. Along the way there are three intersections requiring careful attention and one recommended diversion. In downtown San Anselmo there is a five-way intersection. Proceed straight through and bear left after clearing the intersection. In Olema, Sir Francis Drake Boulevard apparently comes to an end. Turn right and in approximately 100 yards you will see the sign pointing to the Point Reyes National

Seashore Headquarters. Turn left on Bear Valley Road and follow the signs to the Headquarters Visitors' Center. A stop at the center is recommended since restrooms on the point are far apart and often inadequate. A less essential but equally recommended diversion is to bird the central exhibit in the visitors' center. (See if you can find the Northern Saw-whet Owl without having it pointed out to you!)

Return to Bear Valley Road and take a left. Follow Bear Valley Road to its end where it rejoins Sir Francis Drake Boulevard. Take a left and continue through the village of Inverness bearing left at the intersection with Pierce Point Road approximately a mile beyond the village.

Facilities: There are restrooms at the Point Reyes headquarters building, the lighthouse visitors' center, and at Drake's Beach, and a snack bar at Drake's Beach. The towns of Inverness, Olema, Point Reyes Station, and Stinson Beach have good restaurants, inns, and service stations.

Nearby points of interest: At the Point Reyes National Seashore Headquarters you will find an interpretive center and small bookstore in the visitors' center building and, nearby, the Morgan Horse Ranch, Kule Loklo Indian Village, Woodpecker Nature Trail, and several different trailheads. See also the descriptions of other Marin County areas in the Greater Bay Area Birding Spots section.

Special notes: Weather at Point Reyes is highly variable. Even when there are swimmers at Drake's Beach, a warm jacket or windbreaker and a hat may be necessary at the lighthouse. Point Reyes has the lowest average summer temperature in the continental United States but there are occasional warm and balmy days as early as March and as late as November.

Weather can also dictate the quality of the birding. A high fog or low overcast with a moderate wind usually produces the best birding. A wind coming off the mainland is a bonus. A clear day with high winds coming off the ocean is the worst kind of birding weather and many experienced birders will retreat to Tomales Bay or to inland spots on such days. Clear, warm days with little or no wind are generally poor birding but are so rare at Point Reyes that they should be enjoyed for their own sake.

— Cliff Richer

SEQUOIA AUDUBON SOCIETY

A CHECKLIST OF THE BIRDS OF
SAN MATEO COUNTY, CALIFORNIA

COMPILED BY PETER J. METROPULOS
FOR
THE SEQUOIA AUDUBON SOCIETY
July 1984

Symbols used in this list are defined as follows:

W = Winter	December - February
S = Spring	March - May
S = Summer	June - July
F = Fall	August - November

● = species nests regularly

* = species nests irregularly

+ = nesting suspected but not proven

(Horizontal lines separate each family of birds.)

c - common   always present and in large numbers

f - fairly common always present but in small
                  to moderate numbers

u - uncommon   usually present in small numbers

r - rare   present each year but in very small numbers

v - very rare   very small numbers occur irregularly

a - accidental   fewer than five records have occured
                  in each season

This list of 372 species is in accordance with the Sixth
A.O.U. Checklist as amended.
Nesting evidence exists for 146 of these species.

	W	S	S	F			
Red-throated Loon	f	c	r	f	...	...	...
Arctic Loon	f	c	r	c	...	...	...
Common Loon	f	c	r	f	...	...	...
Pied-billed Grebe •	f	f	u	f	...	...	...
Horned Grebe	f	f	v	f	...	...	...
Red-necked Grebe	r	r		r	...	...	...
Eared Grebe	f	f	v	f	...	...	...
Western Grebe	c	c	u	c	...	...	...
Black-footed Albatross		r	r	a	...	...	...
Laysan Albatross		v			...	...	...
Northern Fulmar	u	u		r	...	...	...
Pink-footed Shearwater		u	u	u	...	...	...
Buller's Shearwater			a	u	...	...	...
Sooty Shearwater	r	c	c	c	...	...	...
Short-tailed Shearwater	v	v		v	...	...	...
Black-vented Shearwater	v	r	a	c	...	...	...
Leach's Storm-Petrel	a	a		a	...	...	...
Ashy Storm-Petrel		v	v	v	...	...	...
Black Storm-Petrel			v	v	...	...	...
American White Pelican	r	v	v	r	...	...	...
Brown Pelican	r	u	c	c	...	...	...
Double-crested Cormorant	c	f	u	c	...	...	...
Brandt's Cormorant •	c	c	c	c	...	...	...
Pelagic Cormorant •	c	c	c	c	...	...	...
American Bittern •	r	v	v	r	...	...	...
Great Blue Heron •	f	f	f	f	...	...	...
Great Egret *	f	u	u	f	...	...	...
Snowy Egret •	f	f	f	f	...	...	...
Cattle Egret	r	a		r	...	...	...
Green-backed Heron +	v	r	v	r	...	...	...
Black-crowned Night-Heron •	f	f	f	f	...	...	...
Tundra Swan	v	a		v	...	...	...
Greater White-fronted Goose	r	a		r	...	...	...
Snow Goose	v	a		v	...	...	...
Ross' Goose	v				...	...	...
Brant	r	f	v	r	...	...	...
Canada Goose	f	r		u	...	...	...
Wood Duck •	u	r	r	r	...	...	...
Green-winged Teal	f	u		f	...	...	...
Mallard •	c	f	f	f	...	...	...
Northern Pintail •	c	u	r	c	...	...	...
Blue-winged Teal	v	r	v	r	...	...	...
Cinnamon Teal •	u	f	f	f	...	...	...
Northern Shoveler •	f	u	r	f	...	...	...
Gadwall •	u	r	r	u	...	...	...
Eurasian Wigeon	v			v	...	...	...
American Wigeon	c	u		f	...	...	...
Canvasback	c	f	v	f	...	...	...
Redhead	r	a		r	...	...	...

122

	W	S	S	F			
Ring-necked Duck	u	r		u	...	...	...
Greater Scaup	c	f	r	f	...	...	...
Lesser Scaup	c	f	r	f	...	...	...
Harlequin Duck	v	v	v	v	...	...	...
Oldsquaw	r	v	a	v	...	...	...
Black Scoter	u	u	v	u	...	...	...
Surf Scoter	c	c	u	c	...	...	...
White-winged Scoter	f	f	r	f	...	...	...
Common Goldeneye	f	u	v	u	...	...	...
Barrow's Goldeneye	r	a		v	...	...	...
Bufflehead	c	u	a	u	...	...	...
Hooded Merganser	r	a		r	...	...	...
Common Merganser	r	r		r	...	...	...
Red-breasted Merganser	f	f	r	f	...	...	...
Ruddy Duck •	c	f	u	f	...	...	...
Turkey Vulture •	f	f	f	f	...	...	...
Osprey	v	r	a	r	...	...	...
Black-shouldered Kite •	u	r	r	u	...	...	...
Bald Eagle	v	v	a	v	...	...	...
Northern Harrier •	f	u	u	f	...	...	...
Sharp-shinned Hawk •	f	u	r	f	...	...	...
Cooper's Hawk •	f	u	r	f	...	...	...
Red-shouldered Hawk •	u	u	u	u	...	...	...
Broad-winged Hawk	a	a		a	...	...	...
Red-tailed Hawk •	f	f	f	f	...	...	...
Ferruginous Hawk	v	a		v	...	...	...
Rough-legged Hawk	r	v		r	...	...	...
Golden Eagle *	r	r	v	r	...	...	...
American Kestrel •	f	f	f	f	...	...	...
Merlin	r	v		r	...	...	...
Peregrine Falcon *	r	r	v	r	...	...	...
Prairie Falcon	v			v	...	...	...
Ring-necked Pheasant •	r	r	r	r	...	...	...
California Quail •	c	c	c	c	...	...	...
Black Rail	v			v	...	...	.:
Clapper Rail •	f	f	f	f	...	...	...
Virginia Rail •	u	u	r	u	...	...	...
Sora + ...	u	r	r	u	...	...	...
Common Moorhen *	r	v	v	r	...	...	...
American Coot •	c	f	f	c	...	...	...
Black-bellied Plover	c	c	u	c	...	...	...
Lesser Golden-Plover	v	v	a	r	...	...	...
Snowy Plover •	u	r	r	u	...	...	...
Semipalmated Plover	f	f	r	f	...	...	...
Killdeer •	c	f	f	c	...	...	...
American Black Oystercatcher •	u	u	u	u	...	...	...
Black-necked Stilt •	u	f	f	f	...	...	...
American Avocet •	f	f	r	f	...	...	...
Greater Yellowlegs	f	f	r	f	...	...	...
Lesser Yellowlegs	v	r	a	r	...	...	...

	W	S	S	F
Solitary Sandpiper		v		v
Willet	c	c	u	c
Wandering Tattler	u	u	v	u
Spotted Sandpiper *	u	u	v	u
Whimbrel	u	u	r	u
Long-billed Curlew	u	u	r	u
Marbled Godwit	c	c	u	c
Ruddy Turnstone	u	u	r	u
Black Turnstone	c	c	u	c
Surfbird	f	f	v	f
Red Knot	u	u	v	u
Sanderling	c	c	u	c
Semipalmated Sandpiper			a	v
Western Sandpiper	c	c	r	c
Least Sandpiper	c	c	r	c
Baird's Sandpiper			a	r
Pectoral Sandpiper		a	a	r
Rock Sandpiper	v	v		v
Dunlin	c	c	a	c
Short-billed Dowitcher	c	c	r	c
Long-billed Dowitcher	c	c	r	c
Common Snipe	u	u		u
Wilson's Phalarope		r	r	r
Red-necked Phalarope		c	r	c
Red Phalarope	r	u	a	u
Pomarine Jaeger	r	u	v	u
Parasitic Jaeger	v	u	a	u
Franklin's Gull		v	a	v
Bonaparte's Gull	u	c	r	f
Heermann's Gull	r	r	c	c
Mew Gull	c	u		f
Ring-billed Gull	c	c	u	c
California Gull	c	c	f	c
Herring Gull	f	f	v	u
Thayer's Gull	u	r		u
Western Gull •	c	c	c	c
Glaucous-winged Gull	c	c	u	c
Glaucous Gull	v	v		v
Black-legged Kittiwake	r	r	v	r
Sabine's Gull		r	a	v
Caspian Tern •		f	f	f
Elegant Tern	a		u	c
Common Tern		u	v	u
Arctic Tern		r	v	r
Forster's Tern •	f	c	c	c
Least Tern +		r	r	r
Black Tern	a	v	a	v
Common Murre •	c	c	c	c
Pigeon Guillemot •	v	c	c	u
Marbled Murrelet •	u	u	u	u
Xantus' Murrelet		a		v
Ancient Murrelet	r	r		v
Cassin's Auklet	r	r		r
Rhinoceros Auklet +	u	u	r	u
Tufted Puffin +		r	r	r

	W	S	S	F			
Rock Dove •	c	c	c	c			
Band-tailed Pigeon •	f	f	f	f			
Mourning Dove •	c	c	c	c			
Common Barn-Owl •	f	f	f	f			
Western Screech Owl •	u	u	u	u			
Great Horned Owl •	f	f	f	f			
Northern Pygmy-Owl •	u	u	u	u			
Burrowing Owl *	r	v	v	r			
Spotted Owl *	v	v	v	v			
Long-eared Owl	v			v			
Short-eared Owl *	r	v	v	r			
Northern Saw-whet Owl •	r	r	r	r			
Common Poorwill •	a	u	u	r			
Black Swift •		r	r	r			
Vaux's Swift •	a	u	u	u			
White-throated Swift •	r	u	u	u			
Anna's Hummingbird •	c	c	c	c			
Rufous Hummingbird	a	u	r	r			
Allen's Hummingbird •	u	c	c	u			
Belted Kingfisher •	u	u	u	u			
Lewis' Woodpecker	v	v		v			
Acorn Woodpecker •	f	f	f	f			
Red-breasted Sapsucker	u	r		u			
Nuttall's Woodpecker •	u	u	u	u			
Downy Woodpecker •	f	f	f	f			
Hairy Woodpecker •	f	f	f	f			
Northern Flicker •	c	f	f	c			
Plieated Woodpecker •	v	v	v	v			
Olive-sided Flycatcher •		c	c	f			
Western Wood-Pewee •		c	c	c			
Willow Flycatcher		a	a	r			
Western Flycatcher •		c	c	c			
Black Phoebe •	c	f	f	c			
Say's Phoebe	f	u		f			
Ash-throated Flycatcher •		f	f	u			
Tropical Kingbird	v	a		v			
Western Kingbird +		r	v	r			
Horned Lark •	u	u	u	u			
Purple Martin *		r	r	r			
Tree Swallow •	r	c	c	c			
Violet-green Swallow •	r	c	c	c			
No. Rough-winged Swallow •		f	f	f			
Bank Swallow •		r	r	r			
Cliff Swallow •		c	c	c			
Barn Swallow •	a	c	c	c			

125

	W	S	S	F			
Steller's Jay •	c	c	c	c	...	...	...
Scrub Jay •	c	c	c	c	...	...	...
Yellow-billed Magpie	v	v	v	v	...	...	...
American Crow *	u	u	u	u	...	...	...
Common Raven •	u	u	u	u	...	...	...
Chestnut-backed Chickadee •	c	c	c	c	...	...	...
Plain Titmouse •	c	c	c	c	...	...	...
Bushtit •	c	c	c	c	...	...	...
Red-breasted Nuthatch •	u	r	r	u	...	...	...
White-breated Nuthatch •	f	f	f	f	...	...	...
Pygmy Nuthatch •	c	c	c	c	...	...	...
Brown Creeper •	f	f	f	f	...	...	...
Rock Wren *	v	v	v	v	...	...	...
Bewick's Wren •	c	c	c	c	...	...	...
House Wren •	v	r	r	r	...	...	...
Winter Wren •	f	f	f	f	...	...	...
Marsh Wren •	f	f	f	f	...	...	...
American Dipper •	r	r	r	r	...	...	...
Golden-crowned Kinglet •	c	u	u	c	...	...	...
Ruby-crowned Kinglet	c	f		c	...	...	...
Blue-gray Gnatcatcher *	v	v	v	v	...	...	...
Western Bluebird •	u	u	u	u	...	...	...
Townsend's Solitaire	a			a	...	...	...
Swainson's Thrush •		c	c	u	...	...	...
Hermit Thrush •	c	c	u	c	...	...	...
American Robin •	c	c	c	c	...	...	...
Varied Thrush	c	u		u	...	...	...
Wrentit •	c	c	c	c	...	...	...
Northern Mockingbird •	c	c	c	c	...	...	...
California Thrasher •	f	f	f	f	...	...	...
Water Pipit	c	u		c	...	...	...
Cedar Waxwing	c	c	v	c	...	...	...
Loggerhead Shrike •	u	u	u	u	...	...	...
European Starling •	c	c	c	c	...	...	...
Solitary Vireo •		u	u	u	...	...	...
Hutton's Vireo •	c	c	c	c	...	...	...
Warbling Vireo •	a	c	c	c	...	...	...
Tennessee Warbler	a	a		v	...	...	...
Orange-crowned Warbler •	r	c	c	c	...	...	...
Nashville Warbler	v	r		r	...	...	...
Northern Parula		a	a	a	...	...	...
Yellow Warbler •	a	f	f	c	...	...	...
Magnolia Warbler			a	v	...	...	...
Black-throated Blue Warbler	a			a	...	...	...

	W	S	S	F			
Yellow-rumped Warbler •	c	c	u	c	...	...	...
Black-throated Gray Warbler •	v	u	u	u	...	...	...
Townsend's Warbler	f	f		f	...	...	...
Hermit Warbler •	v	u	r	u	...	...	...
Prairie Warbler	a	a		v	...	...	...
Palm Warbler	v	a		v	...	...	...
Black-poll Warbler				v	...	...	...
Black-and-white Warbler	v	a	a	v	...	...	...
American Redstart				v	...	...	...
Northern Waterthrush	a			v	...	...	...
MacGillivray's Warbler •		u	r	u	...	...	...
Common-Yellowthroat •	f	f	f	f	...	...	...
Wilson's Warbler •	v	c	c	c	...	...	...
Yellow-breasted Chat		v	a	a	...	...	...
Western Tanager •	a	f	u	f	...	...	...
Rose-breasted Grosbeak	a		v	a	...	...	...
Black-headed Grosbeak •		c	c	c	...	...	...
Lazuli Bunting •		u	u	r	...	...	...
Rufous-sided Towhee •	c	c	c	c	...	...	...
Brown Towhee •	c	c	c	c	...	...	...
Chipping Sparrow •	a	f	f	u	...	...	...
Vesper Sparrow	a			v	...	...	...
Lark Sparrow •	r	u	u	u	...	...	...
Sage Sparrow +		v	v	v	...	...	...
Savannah Sparrow •	c	f	f	c	...	...	...
Grasshopper Sparrow •		u	u	v	...	...	...
Fox Sparrow	c	u	a	c	...	...	...
Song Sparrow •	c	c	c	c	...	...	...
Lincoln's Sparrow	f	u		f	...	...	...
Swamp Sparrow	v	a		v	...	...	...
White-throated Sparrow	r	v		r	...	...	...
Golden-crowned Sparrow	c	f		c	...	...	...
White-crowned Sparrow •	c	c	c	c	...	...	...
Dark-eyed Junco •	c	c	c	c	...	...	...
Lapland Longspur	v			v	...	...	...
Bobolink •		a	a	v	...	...	...
Redwinged Blackbird •	c	f	f	c	...	...	...
Tricolored Blackbird	f	f	f	f			
Western Meadowlark •	f	f	f	f			
Yellow-headed Blackbird	a	v	a	v	...	...	...
Brewer's Blackbird •	c	c	c	c	...	...	...
Brown-headed Cowbird •	u	f	f	f	...	...	...
Hooded Oriole •	a	f	f	u	...	...	...
Northern Oriole •	a	f	f	u	...	...	...
Purple Finch •	c	c	c	c	...	...	...
House Finch •	c	c	c	c	...	...	...
Red Crossbill *	r	v	v	r	...	...	...
Pine Siskin •	c	f	f	c	...	...	...
Lesser Goldfinch •	c	c	c	c	...	...	...
Lawrence's Goldfinch *	v	r	r	v	...	...	...
American Goldfinch •	c	c	c	c	...	...	...
Evening Grosbeak	r	r		r	...	...	...
House Sparrow •	c	c	c	c	...	...	...

ADDITIONAL RECORDS:

(Recorded five times or less in San Mateo County and not to be expected).
Number in parenthesis indicates number of recorded occurrences in County. If not indicated only one record exists.

Yellow-billed Loon (3), Flesh-footed Shearwater, Fork-tailed Storm-Petrel, Magnificent Frigatebird (2), Least Bittern, Little Blue Heron (3), Yellow-crowned Night Heron, White-faced Ibis, Fulvous Whistling-Duck, Trumpeter Swan (2), Emperor Goose, Tufted Duck (2), King Eider, Smew (2), California Condor, Mississippi Kite, Swainson's Hawk (3), Yellow Rail, Sandhill Crane (2), Mountain Plover, Sharp-tailed Sandpiper (3), Curlew Sandpiper (2), Buff-breasted Sandpiper, Ruff (3), Stilt Sandpiper, South Polar Skua (2), Little Gull (2), Long-tailed Jaeger (2), Royal Tern (2), Horned Puffin, White-winged Dove, Common Ground Dove (3), Yellow-billed Cuckoo (2), Greater Roadrunner, Snowy Owl, Common Nighthawk (3), Costa's Hummingbird, Calliope Hummingbird, Yellow-billed (Red-naped) Sapsucker (3), Williamson's Sapsucker (2), Gray Flycatcher (2), Eastern Kingbird (2), Scissor-tailed Flycatcher (3), Mountain Chickadee, Mountain Bluebird (3), Sage Thrasher, Phainopepla (3), Northern Shrike (2), Bell's Vireo, Philadelphia Vireo, Red-eyed Vireo, Golden-winged Warbler, Virginia's Warbler, Chestnut-sided Warbler (4), Cape May Warbler (2), Black-throated Green Warbler, Blackburnian Warbler (4), Bay-breasted Warbler, Prothonotary Warbler, Ovenbird (3), Connecticut Warbler, Hooded Warbler (4), Blue Grosbeak, Indigo Bunting (2), Dickcissel, Rufous-crowned Sparrow (4), American Tree Sparrow (2), Clay-colored Sparrow (3), Brewer's Sparrow (3), Black-chinned Sparrow, Black-throated Sparrow (2), Lark Bunting (2), Harris' Sparrow (2), Chestnut-collared Longspur, Rusty Blackbird, Cassin's Finch.

SPECIES INDEX

Dunlin 42, 63

E

Eagle, Golden 34, 74, 79, 83, 87,
 95, 110

egrets 67, 69, 89

Egret,
 Cattle 26, 95
 Great 41, 50, 64, 87, 108
 Snowy 41, 42, 50, 64, 68, 87

F

Falcon,
 Peregrine 61, 87, 113
 Prairie 110

Finch,
 House 20, 34, 40, 42, 46, 48, 116
 Purple 12, 17, 20, 24, 34, 48, 74,
 79, 100

Flicker, Northern 8, 13, 21, 25,
 33, 54, 74, 79, 80, 83, 100

Flycatcher,
 Ash-throated 21, 74
 empidonax 6
 Hammond's 95
 Olive-sided 6, 18, 34, 100
 Scissor-tailed 117
 Western 8, 18, 19, 33, 52, 95,
 100

Fulmar, Northern 16, 22, 28, 38,
 98

G

Gadwall 47, 85

geese 7, 87, 100

Gnatcatcher, Blue-gray 24, 70,
 74, 82

Godwit, Marbled 18, 37, 63

Goldeneye,
 Barrow's 16, 58, 59, 108
 Common 10, 11, 16, 66

Goldfinch,
 American 34, 40, 42, 46, 48, 69,
 74, 94
 Lawrence's 94, 109
 Lesser 34, 40, 46, 48, 62, 69, 74,
 80, 94

Goose,
 Canada 47, 64
 White-fronted 64

Grackle, Great-tailed 28

grebes 14, 22, 27, 28, 41, 44, 50,
 58, 63, 64, 67, 104, 108

Grebe,
 Eared 26, 37
 Horned 26, 37
 Pied-billed 13, 14, 85
 Red-necked 26, 37, 58, 105
 Western 14, 16, 25, 37, 47, 50

Grosbeak,
 Black-headed 32, 34, 74, 100
 Rose-breasted 12, 18, 102, 117

Guillemot, Pigeon 17, 28, 37, 99,
 105, 117, 119

gulls 7, 10, 14, 15, 17, 22, 28, 37,
 41, 44, 50, 58, 59, 62, 64,
 90, 97, 107, 108, 115

Gull,
 Bonaparte's 16, 62, 90
 California 14, 27
 Franklin's 26
 Glaucous 38, 98, 115
 Glaucous-winged 14, 27
 Heermann's 14, 15, 22, 37, 105
 Herring 14, 27, 38
 Little 98
 Mew 10, 14, 26, 38
 Ring-billed 13, 14
 Sabine's 98, 119
 Thayer's 13, 14, 22, 27, 38
 Western 14, 15, 27, 106, 117

H

Harrier, Northern 64, 65, 68, 70,
 74, 87, 91, 105, 107

Black-throated Gray 18, 32, 101, 102
Black-throated Green 19
Chestnut-sided 18
Hermit 7, 8, 32, 101
Hooded 18, 102
Kentucky 17
MacGillivray's 12, 101
Magnolia 18
Nashville 12, 18, 19
Orange-crowned 18, 32, 34, 70, 74, 79, 100
Palm 36, 99
Tennessee 7, 12, 21
Townsend's 7, 12, 17, 18, 21, 32, 52, 53, 74, 79, 100
Virginia's 55
Wilson's 8, 18, 32, 45, 52, 74, 100
Yellow 8, 32, 74
Yellow-rumped 8, 13, 18, 21, 32, 40, 52, 53, 60, 79, 80, 101, 117
Yellow-throated 18

waterfowl 24, 68, 107, 109

Waterthrush, Northern 12, 27

Waxwing, Cedar 12, 21, 24, 40, 83, 100

Whimbrel 18, 37, 63, 64, 105

Wigeon,
American 8, 10, 11, 13, 14, 16, 59, 64

Eurasian 7, 11, 14, 55, 64

Willet 15, 18, 22, 37, 41, 42, 50, 63, 64

Woodpecker,
Acorn 48, 54, 79, 80, 83, 94
Downy 12, 13, 14, 18, 21, 33, 34, 52, 54, 74, 76, 79, 80, 83, 94, 100
Hairy 34, 74, 76, 79, 83, 100, 104
Lewis' 109, 110
Nuttall's 74, 83, 94
Pileated 95, 102
Wood-Pewee, Western 6, 34, 74, 100
Wren,
Bewick's 17, 20, 32, 34, 45, 48, 70, 74, 76, 79, 80, 82, 104, 114
House 114
Marsh 24, 35, 87, 107
Rock 110, 119
Winter 21, 32, 82, 100, 104

Wrentit 30, 33, 34, 45, 52, 70, 74, 76, 79, 82, 104

Y

Yellowlegs,
Greater 59
Lesser 87

Yellowthroat, Common 12, 13, 24, 35, 87, 89, 107

BIRDWATCHING RESOURCES

Organizations

Sequoia Audubon Society
P.O. Box 1131
Burlingame, CA 94011
415-573-7368

Golden Gate Audubon Society
1550 Shattuck Avenue #204
Berkeley, CA 94709
415-843-2222
Northern California Rare Bird
Alert: 415-843-2211

Point Reyes Bird Observatory
4990 Shoreline Highway
Stinson Beach, CA 94970
415-868-1221

Audubon Canyon Ranch
4900 Shoreline Highway
Stinson Beach, CA 94970
415-383-1644

San Francisco Bay Bird
Observatory
P.O. Box 247
Alviso, CA 95002
408-946-6548

National Audubon Society
Western Education Center —
Richardson Bay Sanctuary
376 Greenwood Beach Road
Tiburon, CA 94920
415-388-2524

San Francisco Bay National
Wildlife Refuge
P.O. Box 524
Newark, CA 94560
415-792-3178

Suggested References

National Geographic Society, *Field Guide to the Birds of North America,* Washington, D.C.: National Geographic Society, 1983.

Farrand, Jr., John, ed. *The Audubon Society Master Guide to Birding* (3 volumes), New York: Alfred A. Knopf, 1983.

Robbins, Chandler S., et al., *Birds of North America,* New York: Golden Press, 1983.

Peterson, Roger Tory, *A Field Guide to Western Birds,* Boston: Houghton Mifflin Company, 1972.

NOTES